Structures
of
Organic
Molecules

Prentice - Hall
Foundations of
Modern Organic Chemistry
Series

KENNETH L. RINEHART, JR., Editor

Volumes published or in preparation

STRUCTURES
OF
ORGANIC
MOLECULES

Norman L. Allinger

Professor of Chemistry
Wayne State University

Janet Allinger

Research Associate in Chemistry
Wayne State University

PRENTICE-HALL, INC., ENGLEWOOD CLIFFS, N. J.

PRENTICE-HALL INTERNATIONAL, INC., London
PRENTICE-HALL OF AUSTRALIA, PTY, LTD., Sydney
PRENTICE-HALL OF CANADA, LTD., Toronto
PRENTICE-HALL OF INDIA (PRIVATE) LTD., New Delhi
PRENTICE-HALL OF JAPAN, INC., Tokyo

To our teachers—Professors James Cason and Donald J. Cram

Foreword

Organic chemistry today is a rapidly changing subject whose almost frenetic activity is attested by the countless research papers appearing in established and new journals and by the proliferation of monographs and reviews on all aspects of the field. This expansion of knowledge poses pedagogical problems; it is difficult for a single organic chemist to be cognizant of developments over the whole field and probably no one or pair of chemists can honestly claim expertise or even competence in all the important areas of the subject.

Yet the same rapid expansion of knowledge—in theoretical organic chemistry, in stereochemistry, in reaction mechanisms, in complex organic structures, in the application of physical methods—provides a remarkable opportunity for the teacher of organic chemistry to present the subject as it really is, an active field of research in which new answers are currently being sought and found.

To take advantage of recent developments in organic chemistry and to provide an authoritative treatment of the subject at an undergraduate level, the *Foundations of Modern Organic Chemistry Series* has been established. The series consists of a number of short, authoritative books, each written at an elementary level but in depth by an organic chemistry teacher active in research and familiar with the subject of the volume. Most of the authors have published research papers in the fields on which they are writing. The books will present the topics according to current knowledge of the field, and individual volumes will be revised as often as necessary to take account of subsequent developments.

The basic organization of the series is according to reaction type, rather than along the more classical lines of compound class. The first ten volumes in this series constitute a core of the material covered in nearly every one-year organic chemistry course. Of these ten, the first three are a general introduction to organic chemistry and provide a background for the next six, which deal with specific types of reactions and may be covered in any order. Each of the reaction types is presented from an elementary viewpoint, but in a depth not possible in conventional textbooks. The teacher can decide how much of a volume to cover. The tenth examines the problem of organic synthesis, employing and tying together the reactions previously studied.

The remaining volumes provide for the enormous flexibility of the series. These cover topics which are important to students of organic chemistry and are sometimes treated in the first organic course, sometimes in an intermediate course. Some teachers will wish to cover a number of these books in the one-year course; others will wish to assign some of them as outside reading; a complete intermediate organic course could be based on the eight "topics" texts taken together.

The series approach to undergraduate organic chemistry offers then the considerable advantage of an authoritative treatment by teachers active in research, of frequent revision of the most active areas, of a treatment in depth of the most fundamental material, and of nearly complete flexibility in choice of topics to be covered. Individually the volumes of the Foundations of Modern Organic Chemistry provide introductions in depth to basic areas of organic chemistry; together they comprise a contemporary survey of organic chemistry at an undergraduate level.

KENNETH L. RINEHART, JR.
University of Illinois

Preface

Till around 1950, those chemists working in the more precise branches of the science generally referred to organic chemistry as an art or, if they were particularly charitable, as an experimental science. Because of the history of the subject, such a viewpoint was quite justifiable at the time. Prior to 1900, organic chemists understood very well from an operational point of view the structures and properties of the molecules with which they worked, but they knew almost nothing about the structures of atoms! The theoretical aspects of the subject have consequently lagged behind the experimental aspects; theory was often unable to interpret well-known facts, let alone able to predict completely new ones.

In more recent years, the theory of organic chemistry has become better understood, and with this increased knowledge the philosophy of the approach to the subject has changed. Emphasis is now on reaction types rather than functional groups. Certainly much can be said in favor of the traditional approaches to organic chemistry, which, to the best knowledge of the authors have been used exclusively until the present time. Chemical properties are emphasized in both of these approaches. Historically these were the properties from which chemists deduced structure. Both approaches are still generally used; more or less, both methods have been updated by combining presently available theory with more classical aspects of the subject, as study proceeds through the classes of compounds or reactions.

This book takes an alternative approach to the subject, which is feasible at the present time, and which is followed in all the other books in the Prentice-Hall Foundations of Modern Organic Chemistry Series. It begins with the assumption that the structures of organic molecules can be divorced entirely from chemical reactions. After all, the primary tools in the current routine identification of organic compounds are *theory* and *spectra*, and more often than not one can identify a given molecule without running any chemical reaction whatever. The authors have long believed that organic chemistry might very well be taught to beginning students in the same order of presentation that the subject was personally taught to graduate students. First structure is discussed, and next how it is established by present-day methods is treated. Emphasis is placed on theory, physical methods, and the three-dimensional structure of molecules. After molecular structure and stereochemistry are learned, chemical reactions may be discussed much more easily.

In this text concepts from areas of inorganic and physical chemistry have been used whenever appropriate. The ancient division of chemistry into these different areas, among others, seems to us to be unnecessary, and probably undesirable. Thus, the principles which determine the bonding and structures of the light elements do not differentiate organic and inorganic compounds, and the two classes of compounds are conveniently discussed together. To keep the book down to a reasonable size, however, we have not dwelled on the details of inorganic structures.

With regard to the use of classical physical chemistry, it is consistent with the present approach to discuss thermodynamics inasmuch as thermodynamic properties are certainly properties of structures. A brief discussion of kinetics has been added to indicate the connection between thermodynamics and chemical reactions, but chemical reactions have not been discussed from the point of view of the organic chemist—the topic will be treated in succeeding volumes in the series.

Finally, we wish to emphasize to the beginning student that organic chemistry is three-dimensional. Therefore, while the viewing of two-dimensional structural formulas is convenient, it is artificial and often misleading. The field of stereochemistry was almost totally paralyzed throughout the first half of this century, mainly because organic chemists prided themselves, erroneously, on their ability to visualize the three-dimensional structures with which they were dealing. Whenever three-dimensional objects are discussed and pictured in the text, it is strongly recommended that the student examine models of these objects, so that he will be able to give to the illustration a precise three-dimensional meaning.

NORMAN L. ALLINGER
JANET ALLINGER
Detroit, Michigan

We wish to thank our many students and colleagues who read and commented on various portions of the manuscript of this book. We are especially indebted to Professor D. D. Ebbing and Dr. J. G. D. Carpenter for their many helpful suggestions.

Contents

4

UNSATURATED AND CYCLIC HYDROCARBONS   38

5

FUNCTIONALLY SUBSTITUTED COMPOUNDS   61

6

7

8

1
Introduction

Scientists of the eighteenth century assumed that "organic" chemical compounds, the substances isolated from plant and animal sources, differed in a fundamental way from the "inorganic" compounds obtained from mineral sources. Until the early part of the nineteenth century there was a general feeling that the so-called organic compounds contained a "vital force" in addition to their chemical elements, and that it would no more be possible to synthesize an organic compound from the elements than it would be to convert inorganic materials into a living creature. An understanding of what constituted organic chemical compounds depended, first, on having methods for their analysis, so that one might know what elements, in what proportions, the compound contained. These analytical methods were developed during the period of 1811–1830, mainly by Gay-Lussac, Thenard, and Dumas in Paris, Berzelius in Stockholm, and Liebig in Giessen, Germany. The popularity of the "vital force" theory of organic compounds declined during this period, and the theory was dealt a severe blow in 1828 by Wöhler's synthesis of a typical organic compound, urea, from the combination of two typical inorganic compounds, an alkali cyanate and an ammonium salt.

In 1832, Liebig and Wöhler published their research on the benzoyl radical C_7H_5O and showed that this radical possessed a definite structure and that it went through a lengthy sequence of reactions unchanged. Wöhler wrote to his friend Berzelius shortly thereafter that "organic chemistry appears to me like a primeval forest of the tropics, full of the most remarkable things."

Since the early nineteenth century, organic chemists have devised theories in attempts to interpret their observations. A good theory explains all the known facts in its province and enables the accurate prediction of new facts, which in turn can be verified by experiment. The early chemists faced an exceedingly difficult problem. They wished to understand the structures of organic molecules, but the only means they had of investigating these structures were chemical reactions that led to changes which themselves were unknown. The paths that were followed were tortuous indeed, and the amount of effort expended by generations of brilliant men was considerable; we can only mention a few historical high points here. Frankland (at Manchester), Berzelius, Dumas, and several others all contributed significantly to the concepts of molecular structure. Kekulé (at Ghent) in 1858 introduced the general rules of valence bonds and the pictorial representation of a molecule as a group of connected atoms. He also specified rules describing how the connections occur; these will be discussed in Chap. 3. One other major advance in structural organic chemistry was made in the nineteenth century when Le Bel and van't Hoff (1874) discovered the actual geometry of the carbon atom. After this time the gross structures of organic molecules in terms of geometric figures were very nicely worked out, but the details of the forces which held a molecule together and many of the finer details of structure had to wait until physicists were able to unravel the structure of the carbon atom itself. The ideas of Kekulé and of van't Hoff and Le Bel were essentially correct, although incomplete, and we can have only the greatest admiration for these early chemists who were able to understand rather well the structures of molecules long before the corresponding facts about atoms were understood.

After the synthesis of urea by Wöhler in 1828, the synthesis of acetic acid by Kolbe in 1845, and other similar syntheses in the years that followed, it became clear that there was no fundamental difference between the compounds from living sources and those from mineral sources, and a redefinition of organic chemistry became desirable. *Organic chemistry* is now usually defined as the study of the compounds of *carbon; inorganic chemistry* is, by difference, the study of the remaining elements. It may seem strange that the division is so unequal—one element versus some hundred odd—but there are now more than a million chemical compounds that have been isolated and characterized, and about 90% of them contain carbon. The reasons for the existence of so many compounds of carbon will be taken up in Chap. 3.

The electron was discovered by J. J. Thompson in 1897, and in 1911 Lord Rutherford described an atom as a system consisting of a small positive nucleus surrounded by relatively distant electrons. Prior to this time organic chemistry had developed into an amazingly complex accumulation of experimental facts and empirical rules, but, as stated above, a real understanding of molecules had to await an understanding of the atoms from which they are built: Lord Rutherford's concept of an atom set the stage for the development of organic chemistry as a science as well as an art.

SUGGESTED READING

A very enjoyable outline of the historical events of the early days of Organic Chemistry is found in O. T. Benfey, *From Vital Force to Structural Formulas*, Boston, Houghton Mifflin, 1964.

2
Atomic Structure

2.1 THE LEWIS THEORY

In 1916, G. N. Lewis, in Berkeley, and W. Kossel, in Munich, independently utilized Rutherford's model as a basis for explaining many of the chemical properties of atoms and their ions. Lewis further extended his concepts to include covalent bonds (Sec. 3.2).

The Lewis theory, though simple, correlates many known facts, and even today is a very useful theory. The basis of the theory is the periodic table and the fact that the rare gases are almost inert, that is, will almost never react chemically. Each atom of the rare gases, which are helium, neon, argon, krypton, and xenon, contains 2, 10, 18, 36, and 54 electrons respectively. The electrons are visualized as occupying concentric shells; it takes two electrons to fill the first shell, eight to fill the second, and so on, and as each succeeding shell is filled, the next rare gas is reached.

The chemical inertness of the rare gases shows that there is something especially favorable about a filled, or "closed", shell. Elements at the left of the periodic table, which contain a few electrons more than those in closed shells, are electropositive: they tend to lose these extra (valence) electrons and to form positive ions which contain closed shells. Conversely, elements at the right of the periodic table are electronegative and tend to add electrons to complete their partially filled shells. Thus, elemental lithium (3 electrons, 1 valence electron) and fluorine (9 electrons, 7 valence electrons) react vigorously to produce lithium fluoride in which the $Li^{\oplus}$ ion (2 electrons) now has a closed shell only and the $F^{\ominus}$ ion (10 electrons) has two closed shells only.

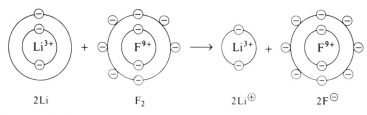

In general, if an atom has only one electron more or less than that required for a closed shell, it is correspondingly very electropositive or very electronegative. If it is two electrons removed from the rare gas configuration, it is less electropositive or electronegative, since the attainment of a closed shell now requires the formation of a doubly charged ion and the presence of two like charges on the same atom is not energetically very favorable.   Thus, lithium is more electropositive than beryllium, and fluorine is more electronegative than oxygen. Similarly, beryllium is more electropositive than boron, and oxygen is more electronegative than nitrogen.

A carbon atom finds itself in a poor position to attain a rare gas configuration by either a loss or a gain of electrons, since either way the resulting ion would have a charge of four. The carbon atom resolves the dilemma by neither losing nor gaining electrons, but rather by sharing them. A more simple example of the sharing of electrons, called covalent bonding, is that of the hydrogen molecule. A hydrogen atom has one electron and can reach a stable configuration by losing it or by adding a second electron.   Both kinds of be-

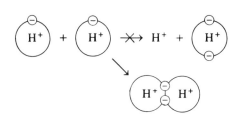

havior are known: $H^{\oplus}$ exists in aqueous solutions of strong acids, such as hydrochloric or sulfuric, and $H^{\ominus}$ exists in such compounds as lithium hydride, LiH. Two hydrogen atoms might, therefore, be expected to disproportionate to give $H^{\oplus}$ and $H^{\ominus}$, but they do not.   Instead they share the two electrons between them.   This allows each of them to have in effect a filled shell, and it avoids the large energy of charge separation necessary to form an $H^{\oplus} H^{\ominus}$ combination.   The sharing of two electrons gives what is called a covalent bond; the two atoms are bound together by the electron pair.

We return now to the carbon atom with its four electrons. Since achievement of a closed shell by ionization is difficult in the carbon atom, covalent bonds are formed. A carbon atom can bond to many elements. If it bonds to four hydrogen atoms, the resulting molecule is methane (CH_4), the principal constituent of natural gas.

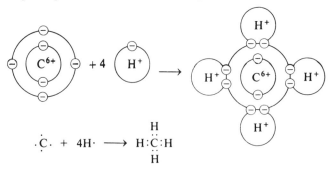

The Lewis structure for a molecule is usually written with only the valence electrons indicated and often an electron pair is indicated by a dash:

$$
\begin{array}{c}
\quad\ \ \text{H} \\
\quad\ \ | \\
\text{H}\!-\!\overset{}{\underset{|}{\text{C}}}\!-\!\text{H}\,, \\
\quad\ \ \text{H}
\end{array}
\qquad
\begin{array}{c}
\ \ \text{H} \\
\ \ \overset{\cdot\cdot}{} \\
\text{H}\!:\!\overset{\cdot\cdot}{\underset{\cdot\cdot}{\text{C}}}\!:\!\text{H} \\
\ \ \text{H}
\end{array}
$$

2.2 THE BOHR THEORY

At about the same time that Lewis was developing his theory to explain the chemical properties of atoms, Niels Bohr, a Danish physicist, was developing an equally important theory in an attempt to understand the spectrum of the simplest atom, hydrogen. It had been established that the hydrogen atom consisted of two particles, a proton and an electron, and that these were of equal and opposite charge. The physics of electricity had been fairly well developed in the previous century, and it was clear that a proton and an electron would not form a stable system if they were at rest: the attraction between them would pull them together, and the atom would cease to exist. Since atoms do exist, the planetary idea was put forth. The electron is of much smaller mass than the proton, and was thought to circle the latter as the earth circles the sun. The electron then would be continuously accelerated toward the nucleus, but its angular motion would keep it from falling in, just as is the case with the solar system. There were some difficulties with this idea, however. It was already an established fact that an accelerated charge would radiate energy, and if the electron radiated energy it would fall in closer to the nucleus. A calculation showed that atoms should last only a fraction of a second before collapsing—and so an impasse was reached.

Bohr then proposed his theory, which made a number of unusual postulates. First, he suggested that the electron could move in an orbit without radiating energy; second, he suggested that orbits could only be located at certain specific distances from the proton; finally, he suggested that an electron could jump from one orbit to another and in so doing absorb or radiate a quantum, or unit of energy. The various quanta of energy would correspond to the differences in the energies of the numerous orbits and would give rise to the lines observed in the spectrum of hydrogen, the relationship being $\Delta E = h\nu$ (where ΔE is the difference in energy between two orbits, ν is the frequency of the line in the spectrum, and h is a constant of nature called Planck's constant).

This theory, like most important theories, did not follow logically from anything then known. It did, as a good theory should, correlate all of the available information on the spectrum of the hydrogen atom. It also predicted exactly the spectra of hydrogen-like atoms, which are atoms containing a nucleus and a single electron (such as Li^{2+}, Be^{3+}). It did not work for more complicated atoms, but it did set the stage for the quantum mechanical theory of atomic structure. The Bohr theory is really a first approximation. It is not quite correct because it assumes that atomic particles will behave in the same way and be subject to the same laws of mechanics as larger objects such as golf balls or planets, and it turns out that this is not the case. The mechanical laws, called *quantum mechanics*, that are needed to describe atomic systems are rather different from the laws which apply to macrosystems (in classical, or Newtonian, mechanics).

2.3 QUANTUM MECHANICAL THEORY

In 1926, E. Schrödinger (at the University of Zürich) published the equation now known as the *Schrödinger*, or *wave*, *equation*. This equation has some resemblance to an equation for acoustical waves, and relates the energy of a system to a mathematical function called a *wave function*. It thus ascribes the properties of waves to particles, if the latter are sufficiently small (as atomic systems are). It turns out that the equation for a given system has a series of solutions, which again are similar to the series of solutions corresponding to standing waves on a vibrating string. While the Bohr theory required the arbitrary invention of mysterious "quantum numbers," these numbers follow automatically from the solution of the wave equation. They are a result of the wave nature of the electron, just as an integral number of half-wavelengths is for a standing wave on a string. The Schrödinger equation is surely one of the most important equations known and, as with most of the other really fundamental relationships, a rigorous derivation is not possible. Its justification is that in all of its applications its predictions are in agreement with experiment. The solutions of the Schrödinger equation predicted the spectrum of atomic hydrogen exactly, although, of course, the Bohr theory did, too. The real usefulness of the Schrödinger equation was in the more complicated cases in which the Bohr theory failed. The Schrödinger equation is a second-order differential equation which cannot, in general, be solved exactly for a system containing more than two particles. It can in principle be solved to any desired approximation, depending only on how hard one wishes to work at the solution. The solution of this equation for an atom like uranium, for instance, would be so laborious that, even with the largest and fastest electronic computer available, to achieve an accuracy greater than that of experimental measurement would take so long that not only would one die of old age long beforehand, but the sun itself would have grown cold and the problem still would not be solved.

Here we stand today: the equation for the hydrogen atom (a two-particle problem) was rigorously solved four decades ago, while the solution for the helium atom (a three-particle problem) was fully achieved only in 1958. Accurate solutions for larger atoms are yet to come. We have the Schrödinger equation, which contains all of chemistry and physics, but we cannot solve the equation. A very careful study of that case in which the solution is easy, the hydrogen atom, has therefore been made and found to be very rewarding. It tells us qualitatively what to expect from the larger atoms and molecules whose exact solutions are impossible, and has helped us develop for complicated cases approximate solutions to the Schrödinger equation which are good enough for many purposes.

After Schrödinger's publication, and some simultaneous important work by Heisenberg, the development of quantum mechanics in the late nineteen-twenties was like the bursting of a dam. All kinds of insoluble and apparently unrelated problems in chemistry and physics suddenly fitted into a general pattern and could then be attacked. The land where the quantum reigns is, however, a wonderland and, as in any wonderland, the rules are different. Sometimes the reasons for the rules can be understood, but often they cannot. One of these rules, called the *Heisenberg Uncertainty Principle*, tells us that the product of the uncertainty in the position of an electron and the uncertainty in its momentum is equal to a constant. This means that there is a limit to how accurately we can simultaneously know both the momentum and the position of an electron. We can know one exactly if we don't know the other at all, but we cannot know them both exactly. It may seem illogical that such a relationship exists: we can, for example, measure the position and momentum of a baseball flying through the air. Electrons, however, are not baseballs, and we cannot, even in theory, make this kind of measurement with electrons. It can be shown mathematically that the Uncertainty Relationship exists, but it is hard to understand it in terms of a physical model (such as a baseball).[†]

From the Uncertainty Principle, we cannot consider the electron as moving in an orbit as a planet moves, because to know the orbit we must know the position and momentum simultaneously. We can only know the probability of the electron's being at any particular place. The electron's location is, therefore, best visualized as a charge cloud, dense in some places, where there is a high probability of finding the electron, and less dense in places where the probability is less. Instead of the electron's being in an orbit of the radius specified by Bohr, it has a finite probability of being anywhere in the universe (although the probability becomes infinitesimal at a distance of greater than a few angstroms from the nucleus) and, in fact, the Bohr radius corresponds to the most probable distance of the electron from the nucleus.

Let us look now at the Schrödinger equation itself, and the solution for the hydrogen atom. The equation can be simply written as:

$$\mathbf{H}(\psi) = E\psi$$

[†] The Uncertainty Principle applies to all particles, of course—including baseballs—but one doesn't try to measure the position of a baseball to within an electron's diameter, so the problem doesn't really arise in everyday life.

where **H** is an operator. The symbol ψ is the wave function, which is called an orbital by analogy to the Bohr theory. It is the solution to the equation which we seek, and it tells where, as a function of coordinates, the electron is likely to be found.[†] There are a large number of orbitals which are solutions to the equation and each corresponds to a certain energy, E. These orbitals are characterized by the fact that they are all mutually orthogonal.[‡] The hydrogen nucleus can be visualized as surrounded by these *virtual orbitals*, which are places where electrons might go.

When the electron is in the orbital of lowest energy, the atom is said to be in its *electronic ground state*. If it is in any other orbital, the atom is in an *excited state*. An electron jumping from an orbital of energy E_1 to one of energy E_2 changes its energy by an amount $E_2 - E_1$, or ΔE. If this is a negative number, corresponding to a decrease in energy, then a quantum of energy has been emitted and a line will appear in the emission spectrum at a wavelength corresponding to this difference. If ΔE is a positive number, the atom has absorbed radiation and is now in an excited state of higher energy. The frequency of the radiation in each case is governed by the usual relationship, $\Delta E = h\nu$.

The part of the wave equation which makes it complicated is **H**, the Hamiltonian operator. An operator tells us to do something; for example, $\partial/\partial x$ is an operator which tells us to differentiate with respect to x. The complete Hamiltonian in Cartesian coordinates for the hydrogen atom is

$$-(h^2/8\pi^2 m)[(\partial^2/\partial x^2) + (\partial^2/\partial y^2) + (\partial^2/\partial z^2)] - (e^2/r)$$

where h is Planck's constant, m is the mass of the electron, the differential expression is called the Laplacian operator, and the whole first term is the kinetic-energy operator. The charge on the electron is e, and the second term is the potential-energy operator, which is a function of r, the distance between the particles.

When the equation for the hydrogen atom was solved, it was found that the series of solutions (orbitals) could be expressed in terms of a series of four numbers, n, l, m, and s, which are the quantum numbers.

The principal quantum number, n, determines the approximate size of the orbital, and takes values $1, 2, \ldots, n$. A larger value of n corresponds

---

[†] Actually ψ^2 is the electron density, or the probability that the electron occupying the orbital will be at a certain place. The orbital itself (ψ) has no simple physical significance, and in fact does not even exist. The orbital is analogous to a shipping lane, a place where we might find a ship. If no ship is in the lane, it is just empty ocean, indistinguishable from the rest of the ocean.

[‡] That is, they do not overlap or, stated mathematically, the product of any two of them, integrated over all space, is zero:

$$\int_{-\infty}^{\infty} \int_{-\infty}^{\infty} \int_{-\infty}^{\infty} \psi_1 \psi_2 \, dx \, dy \, dz = 0.$$

to a larger mean distance between the electron and the nucleus and to a correspondingly larger energy (E in the Schrödinger equation).

The azimuthal quantum number, l, determines the shape of the orbital, and takes values $0, 1, 2, \ldots, n - 1$. This quantum number is a measure of the total angular momentum of the electron. For historical reasons orbitals are usually referred to as $s, p, d, f, g, \ldots$, and these letters[†] correspond to values for l of $0, 1, 2, 3, 4, \ldots$. All s orbitals are spherical, p orbitals are dumbbell-shaped, and the larger values of l correspond to more complicated shapes. Such orbitals can be depicted by various kinds of figures as shown. The shaded clouds attempt to show the probability

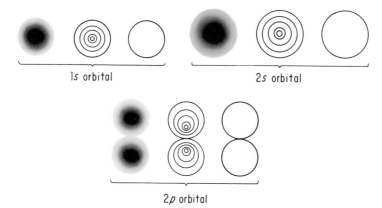

1s orbital   2s orbital

2p orbital

distribution of an electron in the orbital. Contour maps of this electron density are sometimes used, each concentric loop corresponding to a lower density as we move out from the nucleus. More often used for convenience are simple circular figures which can be interpreted as boundaries that contain within them 90% of the electron density.

The magnetic quantum number, m, determines the orientation of the orbital in space, and it takes values of $0, +1, +2, \ldots, \pm l$. Thus, while there is only a singls 1s orbital (the 1 indicating the value of the principal quantum number) and a single 2s orbital, there are three mutually perpendicular 2p orbitals (corresponding to the three possible values of m: $0, \pm 1$). There are, similarly, three 3p orbitals and five 3d orbitals.

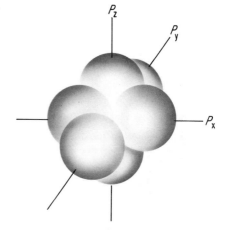

[†] The original meanings of these letters were sharp, principal, diffuse and fine, referring to characteristics of spectral lines associated with them.

The last quantum number, s, is referred to as the spin quantum number. It is pictured as a spin of the electron about an axis which can be in either a clockwise or a counterclockwise direction, leading to values of $\pm\frac{1}{2}$. The spin is best thought of as a property of the electron in the orbital, rather than of the orbital itself. The very important *Pauli Exclusion Principle* states that at most two electrons can occupy the same orbital simultaneously, and then only if they have different spin quantum numbers. Saying it another way, no two electrons in the same atom can simultaneously have the same four quantum numbers.

While the Schrödinger equation cannot be solved exactly for polyelectronic atoms, the general form of the solution is the same as that for the hydrogen atom. The He$^{\oplus}$ ion (or any hydrogen-like system) has the same kind of orbitals as does the hydrogen atom, but the mean position of the electron is pulled closer to the nucleus by the higher nuclear charge. If another electron is added to the He$^{\oplus}$ ion to give a neutral helium atom, this second electron can, if it has the proper spin, go into the same orbital as the first electron. The interaction between the nucleus and the second electron is the same as that between the nucleus and the first electron. The mathematics is complicated because the electrons also repel each other. One can calculate the electron density (or probability distribution) of each electron, and it is found that the electrons tend to be in the same places. They tend to be there at different times, however. If one electron is on one side of the nucleus, the other probably will be on the other side, and if one is close to the nucleus, the other will be farther out. The motions of the electrons are thus correlated, and it is this electron correlation which makes the exact mathematical treatment impossibly complicated. Very laborious calculations using successive approximations have made it possible to calculate quite accurately the energy of the helium atom relative to its isolated component particles. The experimental value is known with an accuracy of one part in ten million, and Pekeris (at the Weizmann Institute, Rehovot, Israel) reported in 1958 a calculated value which is believed to be ten times more accurate. This calculation gives us confidence that the methods are very sound, and if only the necessary mathematics can be devised, the calculations can be carried out for more complicated cases.

In still larger atoms, it is clear that there are the same general types of orbitals as in hydrogen. The succession of elements in the periodic table, hydrogen, helium, lithium, and so on, can be regarded as the result of stepwise increases of the nuclear charge by one unit and the addition of one more electron. (Other changes result from the addition of neutrons and other particles to the nucleus, but these changes are of small chemical consequence and are ignored here.) Each electron is added into the orbital of lowest energy available, and this succession of electron additions leads to a building up of the periodic table. In helium, the two electrons with opposing spins occupy the 1s orbital (quantum numbers 1, 0, 0) in the ground state. In lithium, the third electron cannot go into the $1s$ orbital (Pauli Principle), so it goes into the orbital of lowest energy which is available ($2s$, quantum numbers 2, 0, 0). Beryllium has its fourth electron added to the $2s$ orbital, with its spin opposite that of the third electron. Boron has its fifth electron in a $2p$ orbital (quantum numbers 2, 1, +1. Carbon has a sixth electron, which clearly will also go into a $2p$ orbital. The question arises whether it will go into the same orbital as the fifth electron is in ($m = +1$); if it will, the spin must be opposite to that of the fifth electron, or will it go into one of the vacant $2p$ orbitals ($m = 0, -1$). *Hund's Rule* is applicable in such a case: it states that where two or more orbitals are *degenerate* (have the same energy) the ground state will have the electrons unpaired and in different orbitals insofar as possible.[†]

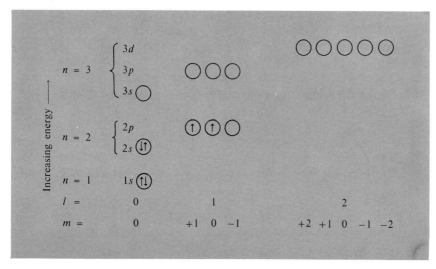

Fig. 2-1 The ground electronic state of carbon.

Thus, the ground state of carbon can be pictured energetically as in Fig. 2-1, where each orbital is represented by a circle and the electrons are represented by arrows pointing up or down, corresponding to positive or negative spin. This state can also be indicated by the expression $1s^2 2s^2 2p_x^1 2p_y^1$, the superscripts identifying the number of electrons in each orbital. Continuing across the periodic table, nitrogen in its ground state has the next electron in the orbital with $m = -1$, the spin parallel to those of the electrons in the other $2p$ orbitals ($1s^2 2s^2 2p_x^1 2p_y^1 2p_z^1$). Oxygen, fluorine, and neon then add their electrons to fill the $n = 2$ level

---

[†] The electrons repel one another, and the repulsion is less when they are farther apart (in different orbitals). Electrons with paired spins repel one another more strongly than those with unpaired spins. These repulsions are small compared with the energy differences usually found between orbitals, however, so they come into prominence only when the orbitals are degenerate (or nearly so).

($1s^2 2s^2 2p^6$). The difference in energy between electrons having the same quantum number n (when $n = 1, 2,$ and 3) is small compared with those having differing values for n; consequently, filled shells are those in which either all the orbitals of a given value of n are filled, or else none of them is. The quantum numbers for the first fifteen elements are summarized in Table 2-1.[†]

Table 2-1
THE QUANTUM NUMBERS FOR THE GROUND STATES OF THE FIRST
FIFTEEN ELEMENTS OF THE PERIODIC TABLE

Element	Quantum numbers of last electron				Electronic symbol for atom
	n	l	m	s	
H	1	0	0	$+\frac{1}{2}$	$1s^1$
He	1	0	0	$-\frac{1}{2}$	$1s^2$
Li	2	0	0	$+\frac{1}{2}$	$1s^2 2s^1$
Be	2	0	0	$-\frac{1}{2}$	$1s^2 2s^2$
B	2	1	$+1$	$+\frac{1}{2}$	$1s^2 2s^2 2p_x^1$
C	2	1	0	$+\frac{1}{2}$	$1s^2 2s^2 2p_x^1 2p_y^1$
N	2	1	-1	$+\frac{1}{2}$	$1s^2 2s^2 2p_x^1 2p_y^1 2p_z^1$
O	2	1	$+1$	$-\frac{1}{2}$	$1s^2 2s^2 2p_x^2 2p_y^1 2p_z^1$
F	2	1	0	$-\frac{1}{2}$	$1s^2 2s^2 2p_x^2 2p_y^2 2p_z^1$
Ne	2	1	-1	$-\frac{1}{2}$	$1s^2 2s^2 2p^6$
Na	3	0	0	$+\frac{1}{2}$	$1s^2 2s^2 2p^6 3s^1$
Mg	3	0	0	$-\frac{1}{2}$	$1s^2 2s^2 2p^6 3s^2$
Al	3	1	$+1$	$+\frac{1}{2}$	$1s^2 2s^2 2p^6 3s^2 3p_x^1$
Si	3	1	0	$+\frac{1}{2}$	$1s^2 2s^2 2p^6 3s^2 3p_x^1 3p_y^1$
P	3	1	-1	$+\frac{1}{2}$	$1s^2 2s^2 2p^6 3s^2 3p_x^1 3p_y^1 3p_z^1$

The quantum theory of atomic structure thus is really a fundamental theory, to which the Lewis and Bohr theories are only rough approximations. It explains perfectly well everything explained by the Lewis and Bohr theories, and it explains equally well the many exceptions not covered by those theories. There do not appear to be any chemical phenomena that the quantum theory cannot account for in at least a qualitative way. The significant descrepancies between theory and experiment appear, at this time, to be only the quantitative ones which result from our inability to perform the mathematical operations with sufficient accuracy.

2.4 PROBLEMS

1. (a) Write the electronic symbol and draw a diagram, analogous to Fig. 2-1, for the electronic configuration of the sodium atom in its ground state. (b) List all four quantum numbers for each of the eleven electrons of sodium.

[†]The electronic structures of the elements containing electrons of still higher values of n are to be found in most texts on inorganic chemistry.

2. Calculate the number of unpaired electrons in the ground state for K, Mg, Si, S.

3. Try to write Lewis formulas for CH_4, B_2H_6, COF_2, NF_3, CO_2, HCN.

4. State the following: (a) Heisenberg Uncertainty Principle, (b) Hund's Rule, (c) The Pauli Exclusion Principle.

5. Define the following: (a) wave function, (b) Hamiltonian, (c) electronegative, (d) quantum number, (e) emission spectrum.

SUGGESTED READINGS

Discussions of atomic structure are to be found in most modern textbooks of college chemistry, two of which are: H. H. Sisler, *Electronic Structure, Properties and the Periodic Law,* New York, Reinhold, 1963, and G. E. Ryschkewitsch, *Chemical Bonding and the Geometry of Molecules,* New York, Reinhold, 1963.

3

Molecular Structure

Organic chemistry may be defined as the science concerned with the *compounds* of carbon. Since we wish to study chemical compounds we are interested in molecules, and our interest in atoms would appear to be only incidental in that atoms are the building blocks from which molecules are made. It turns out that many of the properties of molecules can be fairly well predicted from the properties of their individual atoms, and as our knowledge of atomic structure increases, so does our understanding of molecular structure.

To understand the structure of a molecule, we must know the numbers and kinds of atoms it contains, their arrangement in space, and what kinds of forces hold the molecule together. The determination of the numbers and kinds of atoms in a molecule is a problem that was solved in the nineteenth century, and the method used was chemical analysis.

3.1 CHEMICAL ANALYSIS AND MOLECULAR FORMULAS

One of the most important steps in deducing the structure of an unknown compound involves the determination of its molecular formula, that is, the number and the kinds of atoms in the molecule. An organic compound is usually analyzed by weighing a sample and then burning it in a stream of oxygen. The combustion products, carbon dioxide and water, are separately collected and weighed, and from their amounts the analyst reports the percentage of the sample that was carbon and the percentage that was hydrogen. If the total is less than 100%, the presence of other elements is indicated. Oxygen is usually determined by difference. If additional elements are present, their nature and amounts are determined by appropriate methods. From the analysis, the molecular formula is found as in the following example. Analysis of a sample of a compound (a gas) showed that it contained 75.1% carbon and 24.7% hydrogen. The total percentage (99.8) is within experimental error[†] of 100, so no other element is present. The atomic weights of carbon and hydrogen are respectively 12.01 and 1.008. In 100 gm of compound, then,

[†]About ±0.3% for each element.

we have 75.1 gm, or 6.25 moles, of carbon, and 24.7 gm, or 24.5 moles, of hydrogen. The formula of the compound can be written $C_{6.25}H_{24.5}$. The *empirical formula* is defined as the simplest formula that shows the proportion of atoms in the molecule. Dividing the foregoing formula by 6.25, we obtain the formula $C_1H_{3.92}$. Since atoms come only in whole numbers, this gives an empirical formula of CH_4. Now the molecular formula that we wish to know, the formula giving the actual number of atoms in a molecule, could be any multiple of this, as C_2H_8, C_3H_{12}, C_4H_{16}, etc. To find the molecular formula we need to know the molecular weight. For a gas, this can be found from pressure, volume, and temperature measurements; for a liquid or solid, from the freezing-point depression of a suitable solvent or in various other ways. For our compound, let us say that the weight of a sample of known volume, pressure, and temperature indicated a molecular weight of 17.2. The empirical formula indicates the molecular weight is a multiple of 16.04. The experimental value for the molecular weight is close to 16.04 and quite far from 32.08, so the correct molecular weight must be 16.04, and the molecular formula of the compound is CH_4. This compound has the name methane, and we will study it in detail in Sec. 3.3. By suitable extensions of the methods outlined, the molecular formulas of even very complicated organic compounds can be found.

3.2 THE CHEMICAL BOND

It might be thought that, once we know the number and kinds of atoms in a molecule, the logical sequence to follow would be to find out the order in which the atoms are joined together and then to study the binding forces that hold them together. This is, in fact, the path that was followed historically, because physics (quantum mechanics) lagged so far behind experimental organic chemistry. At our present point in history it is easier to study bonding first because we find that the geometries of molecules follow naturally from bond properties. It should be kept in mind, however, that many organic chemists, by a series of arduous but elegant and brilliant investigations, were able to establish quite definitely the geometries of organic molecules some fifty years before the quantum theory was adequate to make predictions concerning such geometries. Kekulé and his contemporaries worked out the rules of valence—that hydrogen forms one bond, oxygen two, carbon four, and so on—simply by noting the numbers and kinds of elements present in the compounds available to them. The chemical methods by which molecular geometries were determined will be discussed in the following Sections.

There are three kinds of bonds which we may differentiate: ionic, metallic, and covalent. The ionic bond was rather well described by Lewis and Kossel (Sec. 2.1), and is really not a bond at all, but rather a nondirectional electrostatic attraction. The metallic bond is peculiar to metals in the solid or liquid phase and will not concern us here. Organic molecules are held together by covalent bonds, and such bonds therefore form the basis of organic chemistry.

The Lewis theory gave the correct qualitative idea of a covalent bond. It exists between those atoms which can complete their electronic shells by sharing electrons, and it is most common between elements of which at least one is carbon or hydrogen, although certainly many covalent compounds are known which involve other elements. The molecules N_2, $AsCl_3$, and IBr are typical examples of covalent inorganic molecules. There were, however, a number of experimental facts which the Lewis theory did not predict very well, if at all.

For example, the Lewis theory would allow BH_3 to exist, but this compound could not be expected to be very stable because the boron has only six electrons in its outer shell. A Lewis structure for the molecule B_2H_6 cannot be written, and yet the compound exists, while BH_3 does not. Here is how the two structural formulas would look:

$$
\begin{array}{cc}
\text{H} & \text{HH} \\
\text{H:B:H} \quad & \text{H:B B:H} \\
& \text{HH}
\end{array}
$$

If one tries to write B_2H_6 as a Lewis structure, there simply are not enough electrons to hold all of the atoms together with ordinary covalent bonds. Yet we know that the compound is covalent since it is a gas that is very soluble in organic solvents, and it reacts with water, whereas ionic compounds are solids of high melting point that are usually soluble in water and insoluble in organic solvents.

Another example is the triiodide ion, so useful in quantitative inorganic analysis, which has two electrons more than Lewis theory requires. A Lewis structure for the O_2 molecule can be written in which each atom has formally 6 electrons, as it should, and in which each atom has completed its octet. It is known that O_2 is paramagnetic however,

$$
\text{:Ö::Ö:} \qquad \text{:Ö:Ö:}
$$

which indicates that two of the electrons are unpaired; hence no single ordinary structure satisfying the octet criterion can be written for the molecule.

There are many exceptions to the Lewis theory, because it is only a rough approximation. When the more accurate quantum mechanical theory is used, the known exceptions can be pretty well accounted for.

The simplest system which contains an ordinary (electron pair) covalent bond is the H_2 molecule. This molecule has been studied theoretically with great care. It is somewhat more complicated than the helium atom, but similar to it in many ways. Using the hydrogen $1s$ atomic orbitals for each atom of the H_2 molecule (call them ψ_1 and ψ_2), one can write a *molecular orbital*, $\psi_1 + \lambda\psi_2$ where λ is an arbitrary constant, which is a linear combination of the atomic orbitals. Just as an atomic orbital tells us where an electron is likely to be found around an atom, so a molecular orbital tells us where an electron is likely to be found in a molecule. Ordinarily a molecular orbital extends over the whole molecule. The shape of the molecular orbital, or the probability function for finding an electron at different places, usually is more complicated than that for an atom. Such a function is an approximate solution to the Schrödinger equation, and when λ is adjusted to give the system a minimum energy, the bond length and the total energy of the molecule can be fairly well calculated. As with the helium atom, the more refined the calculations, the better the agreement between the calculated and observed values.

The idea of a molecular orbital formed by a combination of atomic orbitals is most important. It permits us to interpret the structures of molecules in terms of the structures of atoms, which in turn we know by analogy with the hydrogen atom. The mathematics works out such that, in general, if we start with n atomic orbitals and combine them, we will always obtain n molecular orbitals. The energies of the molecular orbitals will differ from the energies of the atomic orbitals from which they were formed, some being lower and some higher than those of the atomic orbitals. The molecular orbitals of lower energy are referred to as *bonding orbitals*; those of higher energy, *antibonding orbitals*. It may happen that one of the molecular orbitals is the same as one of the atomic orbitals, and such an orbital is said to be *nonbonding*.

For the H_2 molecule, the two molecular orbitals which are found to be the best description of the molecule are $\psi_1 + \psi_2$ and $\psi_1 - \psi_2$, corresponding to $\lambda = +1$ and $\lambda = -1$, respectively: the first is bonding and the second is antibonding (see Fig. 3-1). Molecular orbitals are like atomic orbitals in that they will hold at most two electrons and only if the

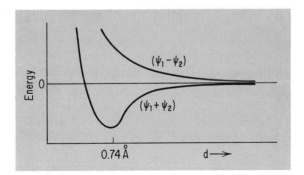

Fig. 3-1 The energy of two hydrogen atoms as a function of the distance (d) between nuclei when the electrons are in bonding ($\lambda = +1$) and antibonding ($\lambda = -1$) orbitals.

electron spins are opposed. In the H_2 molecule in the ground state there are just two electrons, and they have opposite spins and both occupy the bonding orbital. These bonding electrons are more stable than they are on isolated hydrogen atoms, and they tend to hold the atoms together and to form a bond. Conversely, an electron in an antibonding orbital tends to push the atoms apart. The two nuclei repel one another, as do the two electrons, and the two nuclei each attract each electron. The covalent bond is an electrodynamic, not an ionic, bond. The minimum of energy of the molecule corresponds to the spatial arrangement which is most probable, and both the bond length and the energy can be calculated to within 1% of the experimental values.

A simple line was used by organic chemists, long before the discovery of the electron, to represent a bond, and it is still used to mean the same

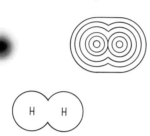

thing although the meaning has been modified somewhat by our greater understanding of the nature of the bond. Various ways of representing the bonding orbital of the H_2 molecule are illustrated. The shaded figure represents the probability distribution of the electrons. Often a contour map of electron density is useful, and the simplest pictorial representation of a $1s$ orbital is a circle, to represent a sphere, as shown. The electrons are not spherically distributed about the nuclei, but show a tendency to accumulate between the nuclei.

The bond in the H_2 molecule is a typical covalent bond similar to those found in organic molecules. It is usually making a good approximation of a complicated molecule to consider the atoms as joined together in pairs by covalent bonds. Each bonding molecular orbital is composed mainly of contributions from the bound pair of atoms. The remaining atomic orbitals in the molecule contribute very little, and the different molecular orbitals thus correspond to bonds between pairs of atoms.

There were developed during the 1920's two mathematical descriptions of covalent bonds: the molecular orbital theory, which we have described, and the valence bond theory. These theories are both approximate ways of solving the Schrödinger equation, and when refined sufficiently they converge on the same answer. The molecular orbital theory is usually the more simple for computational purposes, and it is now the more often used. The valence bond theory is most easily seen in terms of Lewis-type formulas, and is the more useful for certain qualitative purposes. The valence bond theory employs a concept called *resonance*. Applied to hydrogen, the idea is that we can write hydrogen in three different ways: there are certain probabilities that the electrons are both near nucleus 1, that they are both near nucleus 2, and that one is near one and the other near the other. Thus, the hydrogen molecule may be considered as a combination of three forms; in writing this fact, a double-headed arrow is

$$\text{H}\cdot \ \cdot\text{H} \longleftrightarrow \overset{\ominus}{\text{H}}\text{:} \ \ \overset{\oplus}{\text{H}} \longleftrightarrow \overset{\oplus}{\text{H}} \ \text{:}\overset{\ominus}{\text{H}}$$

used, indicating that the three structures are *resonance forms* and not actual discrete structures. It is not correct to say that the molecule sometimes takes one of these forms and sometimes another; rather, the molecule has a single structure which is a linear combination of these forms. The often used analogy is that a mule is a cross between a horse and a donkey, which does not mean that sometimes he is a horse and sometimes a donkey. Thus, the H_2 molecule is a hybrid of three resonance forms, and is none of them. The two forms which contain charges contribute much less to the resonance hybrid (overall structure) than does the uncharged form, so that the latter is the best single valence-bond approximation to the molecule. Unless otherwise specified, the formula H—H is taken to represent the molecule as it actually exists, that is, the combination of all of the resonance forms.

A molecule like H—Cl, which is covalent in the gas phase, can be written as the sum of three resonance forms: $\text{H}\text{:}\text{Cl} \longleftrightarrow \overset{\oplus}{\text{H}}\text{:}\overset{\ominus}{\text{Cl}} \longleftrightarrow \overset{\ominus}{\text{H}}\text{:}\overset{\oplus}{\text{Cl}}$. The form in which the chlorine carries the positive charge is not very important because of the electronegativity difference in the elements. The form in which the chlorine carries the negative charge is, on the other hand, much more important than the charged forms of H_2. The orbital used by the hydrogen atom for bond formation in either H_2 or HCl is the $1s$, while the chlorine in the latter molecule utilizes a $2p$ orbital for bonding. The maximum overlap, and hence the strongest bond, is obtained when the orbitals used for bonding are collinear (see the figure). The electron pair is shared between the two atoms, but it is an

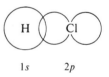

unequal sharing. The centers of positive and negative charge therefore do not coincide. If we look at the molecule as two cores carrying unit positive charges, together with a bonding pair of electrons, the former charge is centered midway between the nuclei and the latter is nearer the chlorine. The H—Cl molecule consequently is said to possess an *electric dipole moment*.

3.3 THE STRUCTURE OF METHANE

Methane, CH_4, is usually considered the simplest organic molecule, and it was established during the last century that it has the structure of a regular tetrahedron with the hydrogens at the corners, the carbon at the center, and angles of $109\frac{1}{2}°$ between any two bonds. The proof of the structure rested on the fact that all four hydrogens could, by various sequences of reactions, be shown to be identical. Thus there is only one

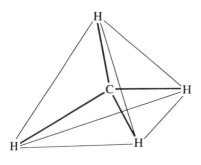

kind of methylene chloride: CH_2Cl_2. If, for example, the hydrogen and chlorine atoms all were in a plane arranged in a square about the carbon, there would be two compounds, each with the formula CH_2Cl_2, for the chlorines could be either on adjacent or on diagonal corners of the square. A study of many compounds showed that the four positions on a carbon atom to which groups might be attached were all equivalent, a fact which requires the regular tetrahedral structure. The correctness of this structure has subsequently been confirmed in many ways.

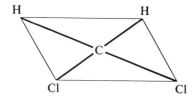 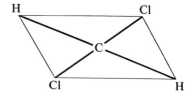

With the development of the quantum theory, the structure of methane was examined by theoretical chemists. The hydrogen atoms utilize their $1s$ orbitals for bonding, as in H_2 or HCl. A carbon atom, in its ground state, has two unpaired electrons (Fig. 2-1). It might, therefore, be expected that, instead of forming CH_4, it would bond to two hydrogen atoms and form CH_2, leaving one $2p$ orbital empty. Actually, CH_2 is a known chemical species (called carbene, discussed in Chap. 7), but it is highly reactive and has only a momentary existence.

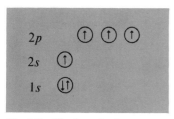

Fig. 3-2 The lowest electronic state of tetracovalent carbon.

The answer to this puzzle was quickly found, however. By the addition of 96 kcal/mole of energy to a carbon atom, one of the $2s$ electrons can be excited to the empty $2p$ orbital, giving the configuration shown in Fig. 3-2. Now, the atom can form four bonds, the hydrogen atoms sharing their four electrons and forming the closed shell for carbon. The formation of a covalent bond results in a decrease in the energy of a pair of atoms, as was seen in the reaction $2H \cdot \longrightarrow H_2$. From the reaction $CH_2 + 2H \cdot$ we can form two C—H bonds, which gives a decrease in energy of 174 kcal/mole. This decrease more than outweighs the 96 kcal/mole increase that was required to promote the carbon atom to the excited state, and shows why carbon tends to be tetravalent. (Carbon monoxide is the only common stable divalent carbon compound.)

At this point a more difficult problem was faced. It appears that there are three *p* orbitals (at right angles), and a nondirectional *s* orbital from which to form bonds (see Fig. 3-2). A bond between two atoms is strongest when the atoms lie on the line of greatest electron density; hence we might guess that the carbon atom in methane would be at one corner of a cube, that three of the hydrogens would be at the three other nearest corners of the cube, and that the last hydrogen might be positioned in any direction, as is shown. This would mean that three of the H—C—H angles would be 90°, the others unspecified. This structure cannot be correct, however, since the H—C—H angles must be 109½° if the hydrogens are at the corners of a regular tetrahedron.

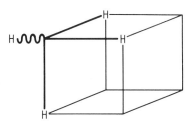

A way out of this apparent difficulty was found by some mathematical manipulations. When the system of one 2*s* and three mutually perpendicular 2*p* orbitals was devised, it satisfied a criterion for these four orbitals, namely that they be mutually orthogonal. But any linear combinations of these four orbitals which were also mutually orthogonal would be equally satisfactory solutions to the Schrödinger equation. They would always have energies in between those of the 2*s* and 2*p* orbitals, and these energies would be related in such a way that the total energy of the $n = 2$ shell when filled would be independent of whatever set of orbitals was used to describe the atom. As a specific illustration, consider the neon atom. The $n = 2$ shell is filled, and the total electron cloud for this shell is therefore spherical. We can imagine that two electrons are in the 2*s* orbital, each with an energy E_1, and six electrons are in the 2*p* orbitals with energies E_2, and the total electronic energy of the shell is $2E_1 + 6E_2$. Now, it is mathematically legitimate to mix these 2*s* and 2*p* orbitals together in any way as long as they are kept orthogonal (that is, in constructing the four new orbitals we must have used exactly one *s* and three *p* orbitals). Such mixing yields hybrid orbitals which are part *s* and part *p*. One way to mix them is to form four new orbitals, each of which is $\frac{1}{4}s$ and $\frac{3}{4}p$ in character. The four are then equivalent to one another and, since they contain 3 times as much *p* character as *s*, they are called sp^3 hybrids. The total energy is: 8 electrons $\times (\frac{1}{4}E_1 + \frac{3}{4}E_2) = 2E_1 + 6E_2$, just as before, and the eight electrons all together describe the same spherical electron distribution as previously. It is like saying that 12 can be factored into 3×4 or into 6×2. Both are correct, but one may be more convenient for a particular purpose.

The hybridization of the orbitals does not affect the energy, electron distribution, or any other property of the ground state of neon, and therefore we can use hybrid orbitals to describe it or not, as we choose. In a fluorine atom the electron distribution and energy do depend on the hybridization, and this can be conveniently seen by using seven electrons and following the argument of the energy calculation used for neon. A moment's thought will show that hybridization will not change the total energy if the shell is full or empty, or if there is exactly one electron in each orbital. The latter case is the one in which we are really interested, because this is the electronic configuration of the carbon atom in organic compounds (Fig. 3-2). Hence, we can use hybrid orbitals to describe carbon if there are special reasons for doing so, which there are.

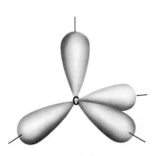

It turns out that if we make a contour plot of an sp^3 orbital it has two lobes, but they are of very unequal size. This leads us to suspect that an sp^3 orbital forms a stronger bond than either an s or a p orbital, because the electron density can be placed more efficiently between the two nuclei which are to be bound together. (It is found experimentally that the strength of an sp^3 hybrid bond from carbon to hydrogen is 103 kcal/mole while the corresponding s and p bonds have strengths of only 60 and 80 kcal/mole respectively.)

Electron density corresponding to an sp^3 orbital

Now all this discussion would be of only minor interest were it not for the fact that the four mutually orthogonal sp^3 hybrid orbitals that can be

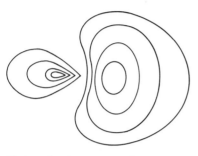

formed by carbon turn out to be directed away from one another at angles of 109½°, that is, they point directly at the corners of a tetrahedron. The sp^3 hybrid orbitals in fact furnish the correct description of the carbon atom in methane. There is an additional advantage in the methane molecule's having a tetrahedral geometry. Such an arrangement allows the hydrogen nuclei to be as far apart from one another as possible for a given C—H bond length and, since these nuclei are all positively charged, the farther apart they are, the lower the energy of the system.

In summary, methane is tetrahedral because, relative to the four atomic orbitals ($2s$, $2p_x$, $2p_y$, and $2p_z$), each containing one electron, hybridization to four equivalent sp^3 orbitals does not change the energy of the atom and it allows both the formation of stronger bonds and the best placement of the hydrogen nuclei for a minimization of their mutual repulsion. Thus, we can describe mathematically the bonding in the methane molecule and understand why it has the geometry it does. Furthermore, we can use the concept of hybrid bonds for an understanding of more complicated molecules (Chaps. 4 and 5).

Before we leave the subject of molecular quantum chemistry, a few comments on the present status of this field are in order. While it is not possible to solve the Schrödinger equation in an analytical way for molecules containing, say, from three to ten atoms, it is in principle possible to carry the solution out to any desired accuracy, and it has in principle been possible for over thirty years. Reducing the principle to practice has been quite another matter, however, for two reasons. One is that mathematical methods are not sufficiently developed to solve the kinds of problems that have to be solved except by approximation methods, which are inherently laborious. The other is that, as things now stand, the calculations involved are very tedious and lengthy, even apart from the approximations. Great strides have been made since 1950, however, and this progress stems from the development of electronic computers. The IBM 709 computer, a typical medium-sized computer widely available today, can perform 8000 additions or subtractions, 4000 multiplications or divisions, or 500 operations more complex (powers, roots, trigonometric functions) per second, and with almost perfect accuracy. A relatively simple quantum mechanics problem may require an hour of computer time, and obviously such problems are completely out of reach of the man with a slide rule. The undertaking of problems which would have been unthinkable thirty years ago is now routine; nevertheless, really accurate solutions to ordinary polyatomic problems by the methods of the present time will require computers faster than the 709 by roughly the amount by which the 709 is faster than the slide rule.

3.4 ALKANES

There are an enormous number of organic compounds called the alkanes, or hydrocarbons, which have the general formula $C_n H_{2n+2}$ and of which methane is the simplest example.[†] In terms of Lewis structures, it is easy to see that carbon can bond to other atoms with which it can share electrons, in particular to other carbon atoms. By joining together different numbers of carbons, a whole family of compounds results. Thus, we have the *homologous series*:

methane   ethane   propane   butane

These compounds are all gases, and the latter two are widely used as fuel. The next higher homologues[‡]—pentane, hexane, heptane, octane, and so

[†] Strictly speaking, the hydrogen molecule, with $n = 0$, is the first member of the series and in one sense the simplest organic molecule.

[‡] The nomenclature of simple organic molecules is not systematic because the compounds were known and named long before their structures were understood. The higher homologues have a more systematic nomenclature.

on—are liquids, also fuels of a sort, and the still larger straight-chain homologues, containing eighteen or more carbons, are low-melting waxy solids called paraffins, once widely used for sealing jars of jelly but now perhaps better known as moderators in atomic piles.

The bonding in these compounds is no different in kind from that in methane: the atoms are all joined by sp^3 electron pair bonds from carbon, as shown by the orbital picture. Each carbon atom has its substituents

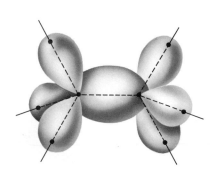

(attached atoms or groups) at the corners of a tetrahedron. For example, ethane could be represented as shown below in the left-hand figure. Perspective formulas (shown below as the right-hand figure) are often used.

There is in principle no limit to the number of carbons which may be connected in a hydrocarbon chain, and hydrocarbons containing more than a hundred are known. One of the features that allows for the existence of such a large number of different organic molecules as are now known is the phenomenon of *isomerism*. Two different compounds are said to be *isomers* if they have the same molecular formula. While propane and

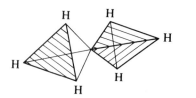

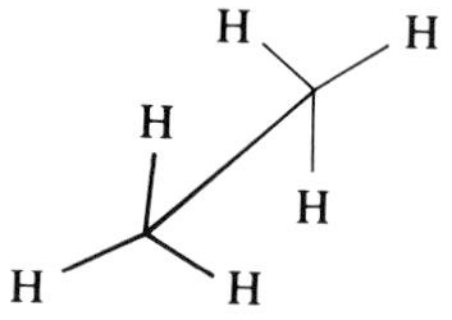

the smaller homologues do not have structural isomers, there are two compounds with the formula C_4H_{10}, three with the formula C_5H_{12}, and five with the formula C_6H_{14}, and the number continues to increase with increasing molecular size, as indicated in Table 3-1. If we write propane, C_3H_8, giving carbon a valence of 4 and hydrogen a valence of 1, it can have only one possible structure. The two formulas

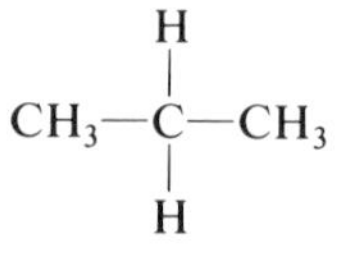

$$CH_3-\overset{\overset{\displaystyle H}{|}}{\underset{\underset{\displaystyle H}{|}}{C}}-CH_3 \quad \text{and} \quad H-\overset{\overset{\displaystyle CH_3}{|}}{\underset{\underset{\displaystyle CH_3}{|}}{C}}-H$$

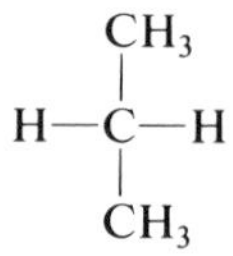

correspond to one molecule viewed from two positions and represent the same structure. The formula

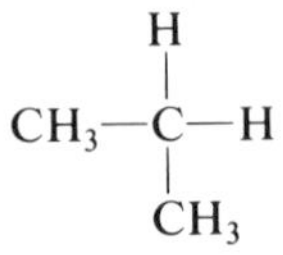

$$CH_3-\overset{\overset{\displaystyle H}{|}}{\underset{\underset{\displaystyle CH_3}{|}}{C}}-H$$

Table 3-1

THE NORMAL HYDROCARBONS

No. of carbons	Formula	Name	Total possible isomers
1	CH_4	Methane	1
2	C_2H_6	Ethane	1
3	C_3H_8	Propane	1
4	C_4H_{10}	Butane	2
5	C_5H_{12}	Pentane	3
6	C_6H_{14}	Hexane	5
7	C_7H_{16}	Heptane	9
8	C_8H_{18}	Octane	18
9	C_9H_{20}	Nonane	35
10	$C_{10}H_{22}$	Decane	75
20	$C_{20}H_{42}$	Eicosane	366,319
40	$C_{40}H_{82}$	Tetracontane	6.25×10^{13}

is also equivalent to the others (although it may not look it), since the four corners of a tetrahedron are equivalent. If it is assumed for the time being that there is free rotation in the molecule about the C—C bonds, the formula C_4H_{10} corresponds to two different structures which can be written as:

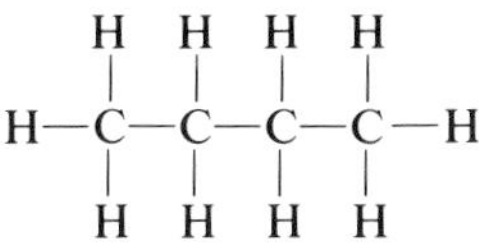

n-butane   isobutane

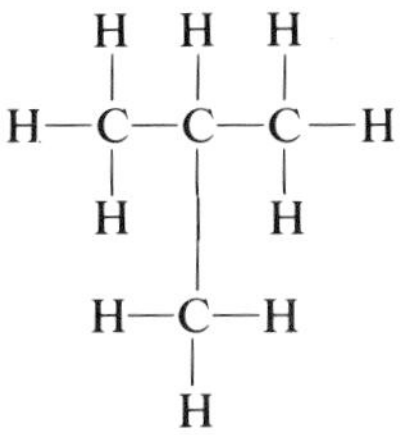

These formulas represent different molecular structures and therefore different compounds. The compound having its carbons in a straight chain is referred to as *normal* butane, and the other is referred to as isobutane; they are isomers. Of the C_5 homolog there are three isomers; a *normal* pentane, an isopentane, and one more called neopentane (or 2,2-dimethylpropane according to the IUPAC system, as described below):

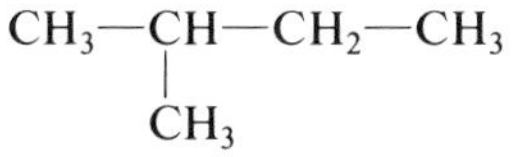

isopentane 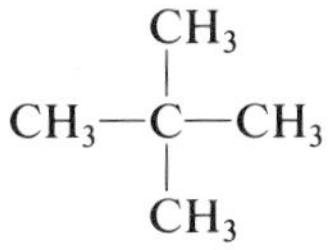   neopentane

There are five isomeric hexanes.

It became clear many years ago that the simple nomenclature described so far was inadequate, and a more systematic nomenclature was therefore adopted by the International Union of Pure and Applied Chemistry (IUPAC). Its first rule is to name the longest straight chain as the base, and to number it consecutively from one end such that the substituents will have the lowest possible numbers. In Table 3-1 some normal hydrocarbons are named. The name of a substituent is obtained from

$$CH_3—CH_2—CH_2—CH_2—CH_2—CH_3$$

n-hexane

$$CH_3—\overset{\displaystyle CH_3}{\underset{\displaystyle CH_3}{\overset{|}{\underset{|}{C}}}}—CH_2—CH_3$$

2,2-dimethylbutane

$$CH_3—\underset{\displaystyle \underset{|}{CH_3}}{CH}—CH_2—CH_2—CH_3$$

2-methylpentane

$$CH_3—\overset{\displaystyle \overset{CH_3}{|}}{CH}—\overset{\displaystyle \overset{CH_3}{|}}{CH}—CH_3$$

2,3-dimethylbutane

that of the alkane by replacing the *-ane* of the latter with *-yl*. Thus CH_3CH_3 is ethane, and $CH_3CH_2—$ is ethyl (see Table 3-2). From these rules, the structure

$$CH_3—CH_2—\underset{\displaystyle \underset{|}{CH_2—CH_2—CH_3}}{CH}—CH_2—CH_2CH_3$$

would be named 4-ethylheptane. A list of the common alkyl groups appears in Table 3-2.

3.5 STEREOISOMERISM

One last complication, recognized independently by van't Hoff and Le Bel in 1874, is a result of the tetrahedral geometry of carbon. If the four groups attached to a carbon atom are all different, there are two kinds of geometry which the molecule can have. These two arrangements (configurations) are different in that it is not possible to superimpose all of the like atoms of one figure on those of the other, simultaneously; the two figures are, in fact, nonsuperimposable mirror images. Molecules so related are called *enantiomers*. In general, such *asymmetric molecules* can occur when there are four different groups attached to one carbon. If two or more of the groups attached to the center carbon are the same, the mirror images are superimposable, and both correspond to the same substance. (This is best visualized with models.) A pair of enantiomers have identical physical properties, such as melting point, vapor pressure, and so on. They differ physically in only one way, and that is in their interaction with polarized light. A beam of plane polarized light will be rotated to the right by some number of degrees upon passing through one enantiomer and be rotated an equal amount to the left upon passing

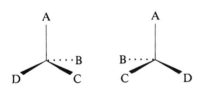

Table 3-2

COMMON ALKYL GROUPS

CH_3-	methyl
CH_3CH_2-	ethyl
$CH_3CH_2CH_2-$	n-propyl

CH_3CH-
    $\mid$
    CH_3
	isopropyl

$CH_3CH_2CH_2CH_2-$	n-butyl

CH_3CHCH_2-
    $\mid$
    CH_3
	isobutyl

CH_3CH_2CH-
       $\mid$
       CH_3
	sec-butyl[†]

CH_3
     $\mid$
 CH_3-C-
     $\mid$
     CH_3
	tert-butyl[†]

$CH_3CH_2CH_2CH_2CH_2-$	n-pentyl (alternate name: n-amyl)

$CH_3CHCH_2CH_2-$
    $\mid$
    CH_3
	isoamyl

[†] *Sec* and *tert* are abbreviations for *secondary* and *tertiary*, respectively. The use of these prefixes will be discussed in Chap. 5.

through the other.[‡] Enantiomers are often referred to as *optical isomers;* the isomer rotating polarized light to the right is called *dextrorotatory* (+) and that rotating it to the left is called *levorotatory* (−).

[‡] It is desirable to have a quantitative way of measuring and recording magnitudes of optical rotations, since the observed rotation of a compound varies, depending on a number of factors. The measuring device is called a polarimeter, and it measures the angular rotation of the plane of polarization of a sample in degrees to the right (+) or left (−). The *specific rotation* $[\alpha]_D^{25}$ refers to the observed rotation of a compound at 25°C, measured with light of the wavelength of the sodium D line (5893 Å) when the compound has a density of 1 gm/cm^3 and is observed in a tube 1 dm (decimeter) in length. If different densities or tube lengths are involved, they are corrected for by using the formula

$$[\alpha]_\lambda^t = \frac{\alpha_{(observed\ rotation)}^t}{length\ (dm) \times (gm/cm^3)}$$

where the rotations are in degrees (positive or negative). This equation is applicable to both pure liquids and solutions, concentrations being substituted for densities in the latter case (still measured in grams per cubic centimeter). For some purposes the *molecular rotation* $[M]_\lambda^t$ is found by multiplying the specific rotation by the molecular weight of the compound and dividing by 100:

$$[M]_\lambda^t = \frac{[\alpha]_\lambda^t \times mol.\ wt.}{100.}$$

Why do enantiomers behave as they do toward polarized light? In general, when we look at a solution (or a pure liquid or gas) of a compound, say methane, we find it contains a very large number of molecules oriented in all possible ways. A given molecule in a fixed, arbitrary orientation would rotate the plane of polarization a small amount, say to the left. If the molecule is superimposable on its mirror image, however, as is methane, it is equally likely that another molecule in the solution will have the mirror-image orientation of the first one at any particular time, and the rotational contributions of the two molecules will be equal and opposite and will cancel out. If one works with a macroscopic sample, the various possible orientations will each rotate the light by varying amounts in different directions, but the compensations will always cause the total rotation to average to zero.

If now we have a solution composed of identical molecules which are not superimposable on their mirror image, and if all the molecules are, say dextrorotatory, the different molecules will have different orientations which will all contribute to the rotation of the whole solution. But for any given orientation the mirror image is not present, as it would correspond to the other enantiomer. Therefore the rotations do not cancel, but they will give some resultant. The other enantiomer would give a solution of mirror-image orientations, hence an equal and opposite total resultant rotation. A mixture of equal amounts of the two enantiomers (called a *racemic mixture*) would give a solution in which for any orientation there would be an equal probability of a mirror-image orientation, and the resultant rotation of such a mixture is zero.

It is somewhat difficult to represent a tetrahedron in a drawing or "formula." The two chief methods of doing so are perspective and projection. Perspective formulas will be commonly used here. Projection formulas show two dimensions only, the other dimension being imagined

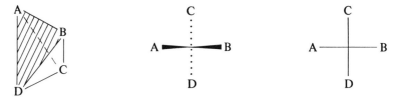

as perpendicular to the plane of the paper, with heavy lines to indicate bonds above it and dotted lines to indicate those below it. *Fischer projections* also are widely used; by convention, bonds drawn horizontally are above the plane of the page and those drawn vertically are below it. In a Fischer projection, then, while

refer to the same molecules,

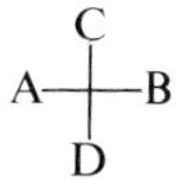

$$
\begin{array}{ccc}
& C & \\
A\!-\!\!\!\underset{\displaystyle D}{\overline{}}\!\!\!-B & \text{and} & D\!-\!\!\!\underset{\displaystyle B}{\overline{}}\!\!\!-C
\end{array}
$$

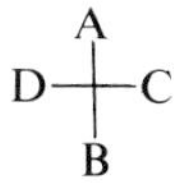

are not identical, but are enantiomers.

If we now consider a molecule that contains more than one asymmetric center, we see that more complicated stereochemical (geometric) relationships are possible. Thus 3-methylhexane has an asymmetric carbon, and exists as two enantiomers (+ and −). These two isomers may be represented by Fischer projections as shown below, which we can call by

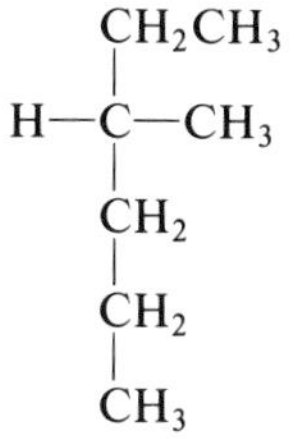

$$
\begin{array}{cc}
\mathrm{CH_2CH_3} & \mathrm{CH_2CH_3} \\
| & | \\
\mathrm{H\!-\!C\!-\!CH_3} & \mathrm{CH_3\!-\!C\!-\!H} \\
| & | \\
\mathrm{CH_2} & \mathrm{CH_2} \\
| & | \\
\mathrm{CH_2} & \mathrm{CH_2} \\
| & | \\
\mathrm{CH_3} & \mathrm{CH_3} \\
\mathrm{S} & \mathrm{R}
\end{array}
$$

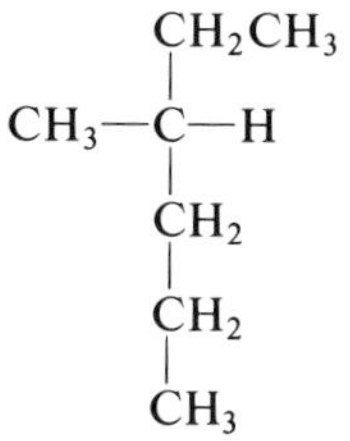

the labels R and S (for *rectus*, Latin for right, and *sinister*, Latin for left).[†] (Note that there is no simple way to tell whether the R and S structures correspond to the (+) and (−) enantiomers respectively, or vice versa.) The more complicated molecule 3,4-dimethylheptane has two asymmetric carbons and a greater number of isomers. If we note that each center has the possibility of an R or an S configuration, we can see that there are four possible isomers, RR, SS, RS, and SR:

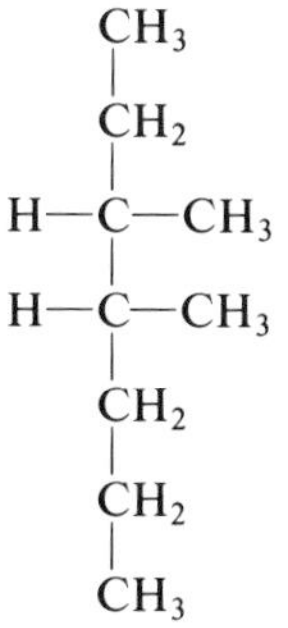

$$
\begin{array}{cccc}
\mathrm{CH_3} & \mathrm{CH_3} & \mathrm{CH_3} & \mathrm{CH_3} \\
| & | & | & | \\
\mathrm{CH_2} & \mathrm{CH_2} & \mathrm{CH_2} & \mathrm{CH_2} \\
| & | & | & | \\
\mathrm{H\!-\!C\!-\!CH_3} & \mathrm{CH_3\!-\!C\!-\!H} & \mathrm{CH_3\!-\!C\!-\!H} & \mathrm{H\!-\!C\!-\!CH_3} \\
| & | & | & | \\
\mathrm{H\!-\!C\!-\!CH_3} & \mathrm{CH_3\!-\!C\!-\!H} & \mathrm{H\!-\!C\!-\!CH_3} & \mathrm{CH_3\!-\!C\!-\!H} \\
| & | & | & | \\
\mathrm{CH_2} & \mathrm{CH_2} & \mathrm{CH_2} & \mathrm{CH_2} \\
| & | & | & | \\
\mathrm{CH_2} & \mathrm{CH_2} & \mathrm{CH_2} & \mathrm{CH_2} \\
| & | & | & | \\
\mathrm{CH_3} & \mathrm{CH_3} & \mathrm{CH_3} & \mathrm{CH_3} \\
\mathrm{SR} & \mathrm{RS} & \mathrm{RR} & \mathrm{SS}
\end{array}
$$

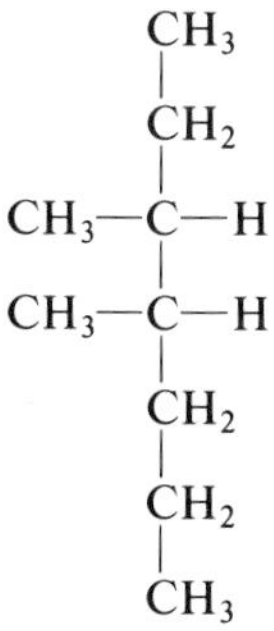

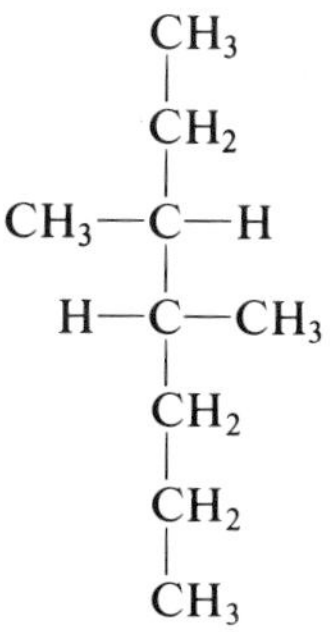

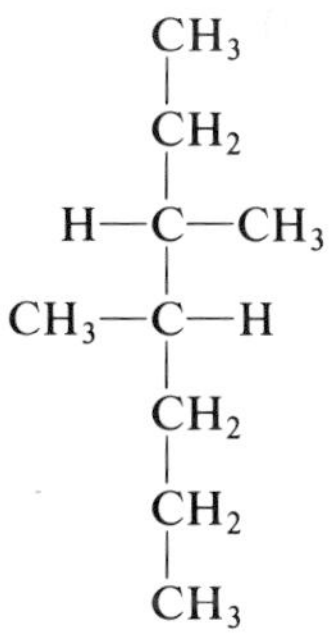

In general, if we have n asymmetric centers we may have as many as 2^n optical isomers. Optical isomers which are mirror images (like the pair RR and SS or the pair RS and SR) are enantiomers, while optical isomers

---

[†] The older literature uses the symbols D and L to specify configuration. The definitions of R and S differ from those of D and L, but are too complicated to take up here. It usually turns out that R and D refer to one configuration, and S and L to the other.

which are not mirror images are also possible (like RR and RS), and the latter type are called *diastereomers*. It is important to note that two diastereomers will, in general, have different physical properties—different melting points, boiling points, solubilities, and so on. Their optical rotations bear no particular relation to one another.

Sometimes, because of molecular symmetry, the total number of optical isomers of a structure is less than 2^n. A molecule which furnishes an example of such a situation is 3,4-dimethylhexane. Here, since both ends of the molecule are the same, $+ -$ is identical to $- +$. The two asym-

$$
\begin{array}{ccc}
\text{CH}_3 & & \text{CH}_3 \\
| & & | \\
\text{CH}_2 & & \text{CH}_2 \\
| & & | \\
\text{H}-\overset{|}{\text{C}}-\text{CH}_3 & \equiv & \text{CH}_3-\overset{|}{\text{C}}-\text{H} \\
| & & | \\
\text{H}-\overset{|}{\text{C}}-\text{CH}_3 & & \text{CH}_3-\overset{|}{\text{C}}-\text{H} \\
| & & | \\
\text{CH}_2 & & \text{CH}_2 \\
| & & | \\
\text{CH}_3 & & \text{CH}_3 \\
\text{SR} & & \text{RS}
\end{array}
$$

metric centers in such an isomer have equal and opposite effects on polarized light. Such a compound is called a *meso* isomer, and it is optically inactive. There are only three isomers of 3,4-dimethylhexane, then: a dextrorotatory one, a levorotatory one and an optically inactive one.

3.6 INFRARED SPECTRA

In atoms there exist series of electronic energy levels (orbitals), and transitions of electrons between them result in the production of atomic or electronic spectra. When the atoms are combined into molecules, such transitions are still possible and result in the electronic spectra of molecules. The energies of such transitions are usually rather large compared with those of other types of spectroscopic energies, and the absorption is therefore found at high frequency, usually in the ultraviolet. Some useful information can be obtained from the electronic spectra of molecules (Sec. 4.5), but other kinds of spectra are found to be much more informative.

A molecule can undergo internal motions which an atom cannot, and these motions can lead to additional lines in the spectrum. The hydrogen atom can undergo only a translational motion. The hydrogen molecule can, in addition, undergo a stretching vibration and rotations in two directions (rotation about the axis joining the atoms, like rotation of a single atom, is not of any physical significance). The rotational motions of a molecule usually lead to absorption in the microwave region (wavelengths of the order of millimeters or centimeters). A considerable amount has been learned about molecular structure from a study of microwave spectra, but the interpretations are very involved and we will not discuss them here.

Vibrational spectra (usually in the wavelength region of about 0.001 to 0.1 mm) can also yield very detailed data on molecular structure if they are completely analyzed, but again such studies are very difficult. Vibrational spectra can also be used in a simple qualitative way, however, and it is this aspect of their interpretation that we shall discuss. As an example, let us consider the H—Cl molecule. The bond holding the nuclei together can be likened to a spring holding two weights together. The frequency of the vibration is similar to that of a harmonic oscillator and is dependent on the masses of the atoms and a property of the bond (or spring) called the force constant, according to Hooke's Law.[†] The motion again is quantized, that is, there are only a few specific frequencies which are allowed, and the molecule vibrates at one of these frequencies. The ground vibrational state is the state in which the vibration has as low a frequency as possible. The vibration never stops, not even when the temperature is absolute zero and all the molecules are to be found in their ground vibrational state. This zero-point energy persists as a consequence of the Heisenberg Principle. The Schrödinger equation applies to such vibrations also; only certain energies are allowed and each is associated with a wave function. The vibrational spectra result from transitions between the vibrational energy levels, and for diatomic molecules can be well calculated and understood. It has been found that the so-called fundamental transition, which is the one from the ground state to the vibrationally excited state of lowest energy, is usually located in the near infrared spectrum, and fundamental transitions are the ones usually studied.

Instruments for the measurement of infrared spectra became readily available only about 1950, so this is a relatively modern method of studying molecular structure. An infrared spectrophotometer is simple in principle but contains complicated optical and electronic systems. A hot filament is used as a source of radiation. This radiation is collimated into a beam by an optical system, and the beam is passed through a prism (or reflected from a grating) to separate the radiation frequencies. The monochromatic radiation then passes through the sample and onto a photocell which converts it into an electric current, which in turn is used to drive a pen up and down on a piece of chart paper. The pen will be at a position corresponding to 100% transmission if there is no sample present or if the sample is not absorbing the radiation. When the sample absorbs some or all of the radiation, the current generated by the photocell falls off, and the pen drops on the scale to some correspondingly lower percentage of

[†] Hooke's Law states that the frequency of vibration ν of a mass m on a spring of force constant k when the other end of the spring is fixed is given by $\nu = (1/2\pi)(k/m)^{1/2}$.

transmission. The spectrum is recorded by having the prism turn so that there is a continuous variation in the frequency of the radiation reaching the photocell. Synchronized with the turning prism, the chart paper on which the spectrum is being recorded moves under the pen in the direction of the frequency axis. The spectrum obtained shows a plot of percent transmission versus frequency. A typical infrared spectrum, that of *n*-hexane, is shown in Fig. 3-3. Note the strong absorptions at 2900 and 1450 cm^{-1},[†] which are the result of C—H stretching and bending motions, respectively.

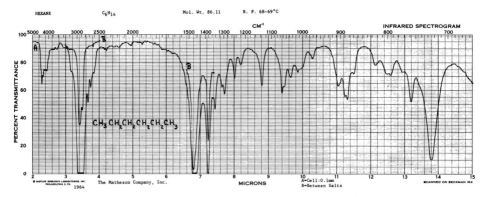

Fig. 3-3 The infrared spectrum of *n*-hexane. (Reprinted with permission from the *Sadtler Catalog of Standard Spectra*.)

As a first approximation, we might expect that in a molecule like ethane, which has six equivalent C—H bonds, the stretching motion of each of the C—H bonds would lead to absorption at the same place in the infrared spectrum. Actually, their motions are not independent, but they couple together like pendulums all swinging from the same bar. The result is that there are six stretching frequencies which are slightly different, and so we might see six lines in the spectrum. Since these lines are very close together it is more likely that we will see a single wide band, depending on the resolution of the instrument. For qualitative work we simply note that the strong absorption at about 2900 cm^{-1} indicates that the molecule contains C—H bonds. Similarly, absorption at about 1100 cm^{-1} is indicative of a C—O bond, and so on.

Most organic molecules contain a number of carbon atoms bound together, and their motions couple in complicated ways. Coupling is usually strongest between vibrations of similar frequency, and because

---

[†]Infrared absorption frequencies are expressed either in terms of reciprocal centimeters (or wave numbers), which are the numbers of waves per centimeter, or in terms of wavelength. Wave numbers are proportional to the energy of the transition, and they are inversely proportional to wavelengths.

of the small mass of hydrogen, the C—H stretching and C—C stretching motions are of very different frequencies and do not couple to any extent. Other motions of the hydrogen in a hydrocarbon are possible, however. For example, instead of the C—H bond's stretching, the hydrogen may move at right angles to the C—H axis; the C—H bond is then said to be bending. There are many different C—H bending motions, and many ways they can couple together. The C—H bending motions and C—C stretching motions happen to have similar frequencies, and they all couple together in a very complicated way. The result is a very complex pattern of bands in the spectra of most organic molecules in the region of 800–1400 cm^{-1}. Much of this pattern is a function of the total skeleton, and this part of the spectrum is referred to as the fingerprint region. Just as a fingerprint is a characteristic of a certain individual, this part of the spectrum is a characteristic of a certain molecule. Therefore, while it is not usually possible to assign most of the different bands in this pattern to different pairs or groups of atoms, the total pattern is useful for establishing whether or not two substances are identical. The usefulness of infrared spectra in determining the structures of unknown compounds will be discussed in more detail in the following chapters.

3.7 NUCLEAR MAGNETIC RESONANCE SPECTRA

While electronic and vibrational spectra were observed during the last century, the initial discoveries concerning nuclear magnetic resonance (NMR) spectra were made as recently as 1946 by Purcell at Harvard and Bloch at Stanford. Progress in the field has been rapid, and the equipment necessary for making the measurements became rather generally available in the late 1950's. The technique is of tremendous importance. The phenomena to be described are limited to those nuclei which possess magnetic moments. Of the three types of nuclei most commonly found in organic molecules (H^1, C^{12}, and O^{16}), only the H^1 possesses a magnetic moment. Most of the work done to date has therefore utilized H^1 nuclei, and the present discussion will be limited to such proton magnetic resonance spectra.

The hydrogen nucleus possesses a magnetic moment which may take either of two values, $\pm\frac{1}{2}$, or to picture it physically, the nucleus is a spinning spherical charge and, as such, generates a magnetic moment. If the nucleus is placed in a magnetic field, the moment must line up so as to be parallel with or opposed to the field. These two possible orientations of the nucleus correspond to two different states, and they have different energies. As with other spectra, transitions between states correspond to the absorption or emission of electromagnetic radiation. Usually what is done is to expose the nuclei to electromagnetic radiation of a constant frequency, and then to vary the strength of the magnetic field in which the nuclei are placed until the difference in the energy between the two possible nuclear states corresponds to that of the radiation. Absorption followed by reradiation (resonance) then occurs. The spectra are usually plotted as radio signal strength against the magnetic field. One reason why such spectra are so useful follows. Since the electrons around the nucleus shield the latter in part from the applied magnetic field, and to obtain the radio resonance signal the applied field must be adjusted to compensate for this shielding, protons with different electron densities about them will resonate at different applied field strengths, and hence one obtains a separate absorption at a different field strength for each chemically different proton in the molecule. The difference in the field strength corresponding to two resonance peaks is referred to as a "chemical shift," and the magnitude of this shift is usually expressed in units called τ. Furthermore, there is a quantitative relationship between the signal strength and the number of nuclei contributing to it. The method is therefore potentially capable of determining the number of each different kind of hydrogen and the location of each kind with respect to the skeleton and general environment. If the molecular formula is known, often the total structure of the molecule can be determined by an examination of the NMR spectrum.

If we look at the idealized low-resolution NMR spectrum of methane, we find that it shows a single line, since all four hydrogens are equivalent. Ethane also shows a single line, with an intensity 6/4 that of methane. Propane shows two lines, in the ratio of 6:2, corresponding to the methyl and methylene protons, respectively. Similarly, n-butane shows two lines, but in the ratio of 6:4. Isobutane has two peaks in the ratio of 9:1. While the low-resolution spectra are useful, it is found that at high resolution the various resonance peaks are often split into characteristic patterns. The idealized low-resolution spectra of n-butane and isobutane are shown in Fig. 3-4, where the signal strength is plotted against the magnetic field strength in τ units. The corresponding high-resolution spectra are shown in Fig. 3-5. The ratios of the total areas under the curves in the latter

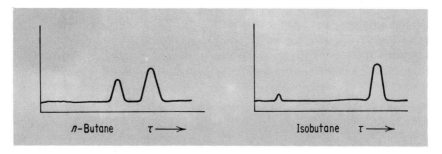

Fig. 3-4 The (idealized) low-resolution NMR spectra of the butanes.

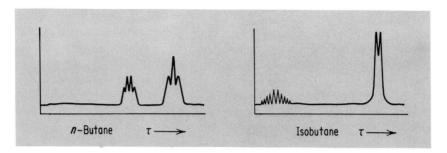

Fig. 3-5 The (idealized) high-resolution NMR spectra of the butanes.

cases are unchanged from those of the low-resolution spectra. The reason for the splitting of the peaks at high resolution is that in n-butane, for example, the methyl protons have two neighboring protons on the adjacent carbon, and these neighboring protons have magnetic fields which contribute to the net field felt by the methyl protons. Equivalent protons do not couple with one another, and protons further than one carbon removed usually exert a negligible effect. The splitting is therefore attributed to the protons on the carbon attached to the carbon carrying the protons being observed.

The neighboring methylene protons can have their spins aligned with the applied field in either of four ways: ↑↑, ↑↓, ↓↑, ↓↓. The first arrangement augments the applied field, the last diminishes it, and the other two leave it unchanged. These arrangements are all equally probable, so instead of a single line from the methyl of intensity 1, we will obtain three lines. One of these will have an intensity of 0.5 and the same chemical shift as the unsplit line would have had. The other two lines will have intensities of 0.25, and will be at lower and higher fields. Since there are three equivalent protons on the methyl, the pattern will be three times as intense as if there were only one.

A methylene proton of n-butane has three nonequivalent neighboring hydrogens (the other methylene protons are equivalent, hence no coupling), and their three spins can orient in eight ways:

The first causes a decrease in the field felt by the nucleus of three units, the last yields the same shift in the opposite direction. There are three arrangements which will each yield an increase in the field of one unit and three arrangements that will yield a decrease of one unit, so the observed pattern is a quartet, the center two absorptions being three times as intense as each of the outer two. The total area encompassed by the quartet corresponds to the four protons of the two methylene groups.

In general, the number of components from the splitting is one greater than the number of neighboring hydrogens, and the bands toward the center of the peak are more intense than those at the edges in a symmetrical way.[†] Thus the magnetic field strength corresponding to the center of an NMR multiplet tells us the chemical environment of the proton, its area tells us the number of equivalent protons contributing to the multiplet, and the splitting pattern tells us the number of neighboring protons. The usefulness of NMR spectra will be illustrated more fully in Chaps. 4 and 5.

Prior to about 1950 the determination of the structure of an organic molecule was carried out by chemical degradation, which is essentially chopping the molecule apart, one atom or a group of atoms at a time, and then identifying each piece and mentally fitting them together like a jig-saw puzzle. With the use of spectra, particularly NMR spectra, structural studies have been greatly simplified.

It should be mentioned that a potentially even more useful technique, which is only now being developed, is the use of x-ray or electron diffraction patterns of crystals or gases for structural determination. These methods amount to taking a picture of the molecule, but unfortunately there are many technical problems to be solved before the methods will be as useful as one would really wish. At present it is possible to determine the total exact three-dimensional structure of a very complicated molecule by the diffraction method, but at the cost of a great amount of labor.

3.8 PROBLEMS

1. A gaseous compound has the following analysis: C 40.05%, H 6.68%. The volume of 3.02 gm of the gas was 2.36 l. at standard temperature and pressure. What is the molecular formula?

2. Calculate the percentage composition of CH_3NO_2.

3. What are the three kinds of chemical bonds?

4. Write the structures of (a) 3,4,4-trimethylheptane, (b) 2-methyl-3-ethyloctane, (c) 2,3,5-trimethyl-6-propyldecane.

5. Write the structures of the five compounds having the formulas C_6H_{14}. Which two show the NMR spectra illustrated?

[†] In fact, the intensities of the peaks in the band are in the ratio of the coefficients of a binomial expansion, $(a + b)^n$, where n is the number of protons causing the splitting. Thus, a single proton split by the three protons of a methyl will generate a signal of four peaks whose intensities are in the ratio $1:3:3:1$ ($n = 3$).

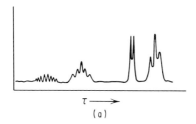 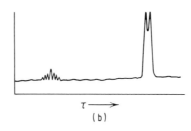

$\tau \longrightarrow$ $\tau \longrightarrow$

(a)   (b)

6. What is the necessary and sufficient condition for optical activity? Explain why an optically active compound rotates the plane of polarized light.

7. Define: molecular orbital; antibonding orbital; resonance; electric dipole moment; tetrahedron; hybrid orbital; alkane; enantiomer; racemic mixture; diastereomer; monochromatic; coupled vibrations.

8. An organic compound was shown by qualitative analysis to contain the elements carbon, hydrogen, and oxygen. A 9.831 mg sample, upon burning with excess oxygen, gave 21.653 mg of carbon dioxide and 11.785 mg of water. The molecular weight was found to be 61. Calculate the molecular formula.

SUGGESTED READINGS

Discussions of molecular structure are to be found in most modern introductory texts in organic chemistry and will be continued in the following chapter. Supplementary information may be found in: C. A. Coulson, *Valence,* Oxford, Clarendon Press, 1961, and G. W. Wheland, *Advanced Organic Chemistry, 3rd ed.,* New York, Wiley, 1960. Further discussion of infrared and nuclear magnetic resonance spectra will be found in subsequent chapters, especially in Sec. 5.6, of the present volume. A more extensive treatment of these topics is found in J. R. Dyer, *Applications of Absorption Spectroscopy of Organic Compounds,* Englewood Cliffs, N.J., Prentice-Hall, 1965.

4
Unsaturated and Cyclic Hydrocarbons

There are many hydrocarbons besides the alkanes. Their general molecular formulas are such as C_nH_{2n} and C_nH_{2n-2} and C_nH_{2n-4} and so on, and thus they contain fewer hydrogen atoms than do the alkanes, whose formula is C_nH_{2n+2}. Most of these compounds will add hydrogen gas in the presence of a catalyst and so be converted to alkanes. The alkanes are said to be *saturated* and the other hydrocarbons are said to be *unsaturated*.

4.1 ALKENES

One group of unsaturated hydrocarbons, whose members are referred to as *olefins* or *alkenes*, has the formula C_nH_{2n}. The simplest stable member of the series is called ethylene, and it has the formula C_2H_4. From the usual rules of valence the structure must be written with a double bond between the carbons:

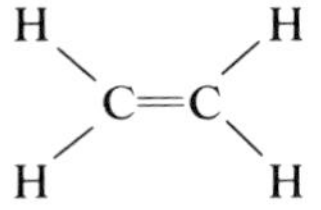

$$\underset{H}{\overset{H}{\diagdown}}C=C\underset{H}{\overset{H}{\diagup}}$$

The second homologue is propene (sometimes called propylene), and it has the structure $CH_2=CH-CH_3$. There are a number of isomers of the next homologue.

The IUPAC nomenclature for these compounds requires, first, a change of the *-ane* ending of the alkane to *-ene*. Then the location of the double bond is specified with a number, the double bond being then understood to be between the carbon of the number specified and that of the next higher number. The longest chain is numbered so as to give the double bond as small a number as possible. Thus, the names 1-butene, 2-butene, and 2-methyl-3-heptene refer to the structures $CH_2=CHCH_2CH_3$ and $CH_3CH=CHCH_3$ and $(CH_3)_2CH-CH=CH-CH_2-CH_2-CH_3$ respectively. The $CH_2=CH-$ and $CH_2=CH-CH_2-$ moieties are referred to as vinyl and allyl groups respectively.

According to the classical theory, wherein ethane can be pictured as

two tetrahedra with one corner in common, ethylene would be two tetrahedra sharing a common edge. It is seen that the carbon atoms and the
four hydrogen atoms all lie in a single plane (the plane of
the paper in the following discussions). Once this was
realized, it became clear that a molecule such as 2-butene
could be written in two ways, and the two written
formulas actually correspond to two different isomers.
The prefixes *cis* and *trans* are used to indicate whether
two substituents are on the same or on opposite sides of the double bond.

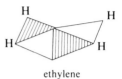

ethylene

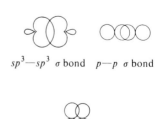

cis-2-butene   *trans*-2-butene

Such isomers have the same atoms bound together, and differ only in their
spatial arrangements. They are, nevertheless, distinct compounds, as are
structural isomers (in which different atoms are bound together). Each of
these olefins has its own characteristic properties, such as boiling point,
infrared spectrum, and so on. Each is superimposable on its mirror image (the mirror plane being the plane of the paper), and hence this type
of isomerism is insufficient to produce optical activity. Isomers of this
type are stable and do not spontaneously interconvert under ordinary circumstances. Such an interconversion would involve breaking at least
one of the bonds of the double bond.

The classical picture of an alkene quite accurately predicts the number
of isomers to be found for the system, but the quantum mechanical picture gives a better understanding of the real molecule. To obtain such a
picture we must go back to the orbitals from which the bonds are formed.
In the case of methane, the carbon atom had one $2s$ and three $2p$ orbitals
which were hybridized to form four sp^3 orbitals. As was mentioned
earlier, there are many other kinds of hybrids which can be formed (an
infinite number, actually); it is only necessary that the four hybrid orbitals
be mutually orthogonal and add up to a total of one s and three p orbitals.
In a particular molecule, the hybridization which will actually be found
is that which will lead to the lowest energy, and usually this means that
hybridization which yields the strongest bonds.

Two sp^3 hybridized carbons can form a strong
bond because the overlap between the orbitals is
large at the proper internuclear distance. Such a
bond, in which the principal axis of electron
density lies along the bond, is usually called a σ
bond, and all ordinary single bonds are of this
type. Similarly, two $2p$ orbitals can form a σ
bond by coming together in a collinear fashion
but, as was mentioned earlier, the sp^3—sp^3 bond
is much stronger than the p—p σ bond. In addi-

sp^3—sp^3 σ bond p—p σ bond

p—p π bond

tion, it is possible to put the *p* orbitals together with their axes parallel instead of collinear, and such a bond is called a π bond. At ordinary bond distances, the π bond is considerably weaker than the corresponding σ bond.

Upon inquiring into the different kinds of hybrid orbitals that could exist for carbon and be used for bonding in ethylene, it was found that

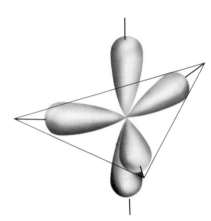

one *p* orbital could be left alone (say p_z) and the other two *p* orbitals could be combined with the *s* orbital to yield three equivalent hybrid orbitals, which this time are sp^2 in character. The shape of an sp^2 orbital is rather similar to that of an sp^3 orbital: there is a large electron density on one side of the nucleus and a small density on the other side. The three sp^2 orbitals lie with their axes at 120° to one another in the *x-y* plane, and the fourth (p_z) orbital is perpendicular to this plane. Such a system of orbitals is well suited to the bonding found in a molecule like ethylene, since a strong σ bond and a weaker π bond can simultaneously be formed between the carbons, and the H—C—H angles are 120°. Note that for effective overlap between the two $2p_z$ orbitals, the whole molecule must be planar. To rotate one end of the molecule with respect to the other through 90° about the C—C σ bond, as is necessary for the interconversion of *cis* and *trans* isomers,

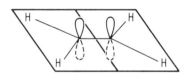
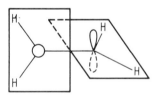

requires that the two $2p_z$ orbitals become orthogonal. This amounts to breaking the π bond. Such a process, of course, requires a lot of energy, which explains why *cis* and *trans* isomers are not interconvertible under ordinary conditions.

The strength of the bond of a hydrogen molecule can be defined as the amount of energy that must be added to break the bond and cause the molecule to dissociate into separate atoms. The strength of a given bond in a more complicated molecule can be imagined similarly; it is the energy required to break the bond homolytically.[†] A C—C bond has a

---

[†] *Homolytic* cleavage of an electron pair bond gives each fragment one electron. If one fragment gets both electrons, the cleavage is *heterolytic*.

strength of 83 kcal/mole.[†] We can predict that, since the π bond is not as strong as the σ bond, the C=C bond would have a strength of something less than twice this value (the C=C bond strength is 146 kcal/mole). The π bond of ethylene is more easily broken than any of the σ bonds, and the chemical reactions of the compound ordinarily involve the π bond.

The electron density due to the σ component of the double bond in ethylene is similar to that in the hydrogen molecule, being highest around the nuclei and along the internuclear axis; on the other hand, the π bond's electron density is greatest above and below the plane of the nuclei, yielding a total electron density that gives an elliptical cross section perpendicular to the C—C axis.

The quantum mechanical picture makes one prediction that differs significantly from that of the tetrahedral model. In the tetrahedral model the H—C—H bond angle is $109\frac{1}{2}°$, whereas for sp^2 hybrid orbitals this angle is 120°. (Actually, there is no necessity for the σ bonds to be all exactly sp^2; one or two of them can contain slightly more p character, as $sp^{2.05}$ for example, if the others contain a correspondingly less amount, and such small changes in hybridization are accompanied by small changes in bond angle.) Since the σ bonds to the two hydrogens are different from the σ bond to carbon, there was, historically, no reason to anticipate an exact 120° bond angle, but it was expected that the angle would be close to that value (the best experimental value for the H—C—H angle in ethylene is $117 \pm 1°$) and, except for very accurate work, the sp^2 hybrid is the approximation used.

The length of a bond, or the (average) distance between two nuclei bound together, can be determined experimentally by x-ray diffraction or from infrared spectra or in various other ways. It is found that the bond length of a single σ bond between a pair of atoms is almost a constant for a given atomic pair, and it does not depend to any great extent on the environment. Thus, a C—H bond is 1.09 Å long in methane, 1.07 Å long in ethylene, and it has a very similar length in almost any other molecule in which it is found. A C—C single bond, similarly, has a length of just about 1.54 Å in ethane or in propane or in any other simple hydrocarbon. The carbon-carbon double bond in ethylene is only about 1.33 Å long. If we imagine the two carbon nuclei in ethane as being pulled together by two electrons to a certain equilibrium distance, it is reasonable that the four electrons in ethylene would pull them together more tightly. A single bond is sometimes said to have a bond order of 1, while a double bond has a bond order of 2.[‡] It is true in general that, as

---

[†] These bond strengths cannot usually be experimentally determined directly in complicated molecules, but are found in roundabout ways. They are average values, and the actual values vary slightly from one molecule to another.

[‡] Fractional bond orders will be discussed in Sec. 4.3.

the order of a bond between a given pair of atoms increases, the bond strength also increases and the bond length decreases.

The infrared spectra of alkenes are rather revealing. The C—H bond is a little stronger when the carbon is sp^2 than when it is sp^3 and, if other things remain constant, the stronger bond has the higher vibrational frequency. Hence the infrared spectrum of a compound like propene shows an intense C—H stretching band from its methyl group, and a band of feeble intensity at slightly higher frequency due to its olefinic hydrogens.[†] Certain other bands in the spectrum are of greater interest, however. The carbon-carbon double bond is very much stronger than the carbon-carbon single bond, and the double bond stretching leads to adsorption in the vicinity of 1650 cm^{-1}, in a part of the spectrum which is free from absorption in alkanes. The identification of a compound as an olefin from the presence of this band is therefore usually easy, if the substitution around it is not too symmetrical. Moreover, the arrangement of substituents about the double bond can usually be deduced from an examination of the infrared spectrum. The bending of the olefinic hydrogen(s) perpendicular to the olefinic plane leads to strong bands in the 700 to 1000 cm^{-1} region, which are usually easy to identify. The bending motions of these olefinic hydrogens couple together, and produce characteristically different patterns, depending on the number and geometrical arrangement of the hydrogens. Thus, a *trans* disubstituted olefin absorbs at about 960 cm^{-1} and the *cis* isomer absorbs near 690 cm^{-1}. The nature of the substituents is of little importance, since it is the olefinic hydrogens that give the characteristic absorption. An olefin of the type $R_2C{=}CH_2$ shows one band at 890 cm^{-1} whereas a trisubstituted olefin ($R_2C{=}CHR$) absorbs at 810 cm^{-1} and a monosubstituted one shows two bands at 910 and 990 cm^{-1}. A tetrasubstituted olefin, of course, does not show this type of absorption.

4.2 ALKYNES

Another homologous series of unsaturated hydrocarbons has the formula C_nH_{2n-2}. The first member of the series is acetylene, H—C≡C—H. The succeeding homologues are named by changing the *-ane* suffix of the alkane to *-yne*, and the next few members are propyne, butyne (of which there are two isomers), pentyne (again two isomers), and so on. The classical picture of the triply bound carbons of acetylene is that of two tetrahedra with one face in common and an H—C—C—H system lying along a single axis.

[†] The intensities of infrared bands are somewhat hard to predict, and in this respect are quite different from NMR spectra. In the infrared, the intensity is higher the greater the change in dipole moment during the vibration. Thus, polar bonds tend to give more intense bands than hydrocarbons, and vibrations across a center of symmetry (like the stretching of the double bond in ethylene) tend to be very weak.

$$H-C\equiv C-CH_3 \qquad H-C\equiv C-CH_2-CH_3 \qquad CH_3-C\equiv C-CH_3$$

propyne   1-butyne   2-butyne

The C≡C bond is said to have a bond order of 3. It is stronger (200 kcal/mole) and shorter (1.20 Å) than the double bond, in line with the discussion in Sec. 4.1. The quantum mechanical picture also predicts a linear molecule. The bonding orbitals directed toward carbon or hydrogen are *sp* hybrids, the remaining two $2p$ orbitals on each carbon forming two π bonds which are orthogonal to each other and to the σ system. The triple bond is ellipsoidally symmetrical: that is, the two π bonds together give an electron cloud which has a tubular cross section perpendicular to the σ bond. On the C—C axis, where the π electron density is zero, the σ electron density is very high, and the cross section

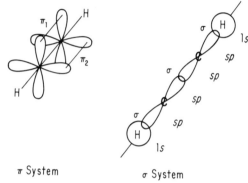

π System   σ System

of the total electron density looks like the cross section of a $1s$ orbital. The total density of the bonding electrons is highest on the C—C axis and falls off smoothly with the distance from the axis.

One of the most conspicuous properties of terminal acetylenes is that they are weakly acidic. They are less acidic than water, but will react with stronger bases (sodamide, for example) to form an acetylide ion. The hydrogens on ethylene are less acidic than those on acetylene by many powers of ten, and those on methane are among the least acidic known. The dissociation constants are as follows:

pK[†]

$$H-C\equiv C-H \;\rightleftharpoons\; H-C\equiv C^{\ominus} \;+\; H^{\oplus} \quad 21$$

$$\begin{array}{c} H \\[-2pt] \diagdown \\ C=C \\[-2pt] \diagup \quad \diagdown \\ H \qquad H \end{array} \begin{array}{c} H \\[-2pt] \diagup \\ \\ \diagdown \\ H \end{array} \;\rightleftharpoons\; H_2C=C^{\ominus}-H \;+\; H^{\oplus} \quad 50$$

$$H_3C-H \;\rightleftharpoons\; H_3C^{\ominus} \;+\; H^{\oplus} \quad 84$$

This order of acidity can be understood in terms of the orbitals involved in the anions, since the C—H bonds broken are similar in energy in each case and the protons formed are identical.

An electron in a $2p$ orbital on carbon is, on the average, at a greater distance from the nucleus than is an electron in a $2s$ orbital. Thus, the more *s* character there is in a hybrid orbital, the lower the energy of the

[†] pK means −log K; thus, a pK of 21 corresponds to $K = 10^{-21}$.

electron in that orbital. When the anion has its electron pair in an *sp* orbital, the energy is lower than in an sp^2 orbital, which in turn is lower than in an sp^3 orbital. The anions formed from the hydrocarbons by ionization are thus of decreasing stability in the following order: acetylide > vinyl > methyl.

The infrared spectrum of an acetylene shows some very characteristic features. The carbon-carbon triple bond is stronger than the double bond, and its presence leads to absorption near 2200 cm^{-1}. The band is usually very weak except in terminal acetylenes. Terminal acetylenes also show the absorption of the strong C—H bond to *sp* carbon at 3300 cm^{-1}; these two bands in infrared spectra make it easy to identify terminal acetylenes.

We might now construct a small diagram outlining the infrared spectra of hydrocarbons (Fig. 4-1). The C—H stretching absorption occurs at

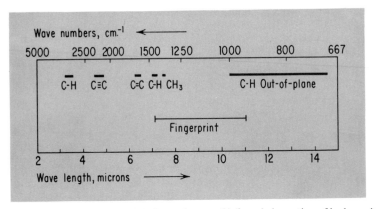

Fig. 4-1 General types of infrared absorption of hydrocarbons.

2900 to 3300 cm^{-1}, the acetylenes being at the higher end of the range. Triple bonds, then, absorb at 2100 to 2300 cm^{-1}, double bonds at 1600 to 1700 cm^{-1}, and most other single bonds below 1430 cm^{-1}. The C—H bending absorption leads to a strong band at 1450 cm^{-1}, and this is present in essentially all organic molecules. A methyl group absorbs at 1380 cm^{-1}, and this absorption is also usually present in organic molecules. The fingerprint region extends from 900 to 1400 cm^{-1} and the olefinic C—H out-of-plane bending absorptions are found from 700 to 1000 cm^{-1}.

The infrared spectrum of 2-ethyl-1-hexene is shown in Fig. 4-2 and illustrates many of these features (see also Secs. 3.6 and 5.6).

The NMR spectra of the olefins show useful characteristics, and will be discussed in Secs. 4.4 and 5.6.

4.3 CONJUGATED UNSATURATION

It is perfectly possible that two or three or more multiple bonds exist in the same molecule. Examples of such structures are 1,5-hexadiene

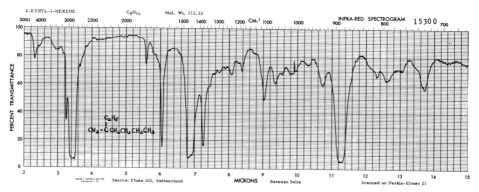

Fig. 4-2 The infrared spectrum of 2-ethyl-1-hexene. (Reprinted with permission from the *Sadtler Catalog of Infrared Spectra*.)

$(CH_2\!\!=\!\!CHCH_2CH_2CH\!\!=\!\!CH_2)$ and 1-hexen-5-yne $(CH_2\!\!=\!\!CH\!-\!CH_2\!-$ $CH_2\!-\!C\!\!\equiv\!\!CH)$. Structures in which the multiple bonds are separated by two or more single bonds have no special properties, the two unsaturated moieties behaving essentially as though they were located in separate molecules.

When two multiple bonds are separated by one single bond, the unsaturated system is said to be *conjugated*, and it does possess special properties. The special nature of conjugated systems is most easily seen from the molecular orbital picture of the molecule, and 1,3-butadiene $(CH_2\!\!=\!\!CH\!-\!CH\!\!=\!\!CH_2)$ can be considered as an example:

We can see that the two $2p$ orbitals of atoms 1 and 2 overlap to form a π bond as usual, similarly with atoms 3 and 4. We can also see that there is π-bond character between atoms 2 and 3, a fact which is not apparent from the usual structural formula. If we write the ionic resonance forms, together with the covalent form, we again conclude that there is some double-bond character between atoms 2 and 3.

$$CH_2\!\!=\!\!CH\!-\!CH\!\!=\!\!CH_2 \qquad\qquad \overset{\ominus}{C}H_2\!-\!CH\!\!=\!\!CH\!-\!\overset{\oplus}{C}H_2$$

$$\overset{\oplus}{C}H_2\!-\!CH\!\!=\!\!CH\!-\!CH_2 \qquad\qquad \overset{\ominus}{C}H_2\!-\!\overset{\oplus}{C}H\!-\!CH\!\!=\!\!CH_2 \text{ etc.}$$

We can still write the several resonance forms which involve charge separation only within a single olefinic linkage, but the two forms which involve both linkages simultaneously, as shown, present a special phenomenon peculiar to conjugated dienes. The molecular orbital picture seems to suggest that there is as much double-bond character between atoms 2 and 3 as between 1 and 2, but actual numerical calculations show that this is not true. There is, in fact, only a small amount of double-bond character between atoms 2 and 3, so the bond orders between carbons 1 and 2 and between 2 and 3 are slightly less than 2 and more than 1, respectively. Experimentally, the numerical calculations are confirmed by measurement of the barrier to rotation about atoms 2 and 3. This energy barrier is about 5 kcal/mole, while that about the double bond in ethylene is 60 kcal/mole. Thus, to break the "double bond" between atoms 2 and 3 requires less than a tenth the energy required to break a real double bond. Isomers that differ by having *cis* or *trans* arrangements about the 2-3 bond are easily interconvertible at room temperature. They are referred to as *s-cis* or *s-trans* isomers (*s* for single bond); they cannot be isolated separately in simple cases, but more complicated molecules having this type of isomerism are known.

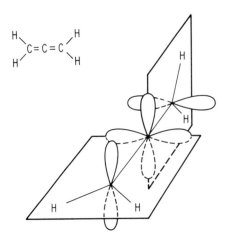

$s\text{-}trans$ $s\text{-}cis$

The experimental bond lengths in butadiene are for $C_{1\text{-}2}$ 1.33 Å and for $C_{2\text{-}3}$ 1.48 Å. The double bond is supposedly a little longer than in ethylene (since the bond order is lower), but the difference is too small to detect experimentally. The $C_{2\text{-}3}$ bond is much shorter than the C—C bond in ethane (1.54 Å), however; this bond shortening is thought to be due in part to the increased bond order and in part to the fact that the σ bond is made up of sp^2 hybrids, while in ethane the hybrids are sp^3. There are reasons for believing the latter might lead to a slightly longer bond even if the bond orders were the same.

One further fundamental type of diene system is known, the simplest example of which is 1,2-propadiene. This compound has the trivial name allene, and compounds having systems like it are often referred to as allenes. The double bonds are not conjugated, and the compounds do not show the special properties of conjugated systems. The central carbon has two *sp* hybrid orbitals, directed 180° from one another toward the end carbons, and two perpendicular *2p* orbitals. The end carbons are sp^2-hybridized, and each forms a σ bond and a π bond to the central carbon, as indicated in the figure. The π components of the two double bonds are therefore mutually orthogonal, and they have little effect on one another. The olefinic linkage in an allene is hybridized somewhat as in acetylene, and it is not surprising that allenes show absorption in the infrared spectrum near 1950 cm^{-1}, which is between the usual C=C and C≡C stretching regions.

The stereochemistry of the allenes is rather different from that of ordinary olefins which, being coplanar, exhibit *cis-trans* isomerism. In allenes the two end carbons and their two attached substituents lie in perpendicular planes. Hence, a molecule which has two different substituents on each end (the ends can be the same or different), such as 2,3-pentadiene, does not have *cis-trans* isomers, but optical isomers. The geometry shown for 2,3-pentadiene corresponds to an optically active compound; it is not superimposable on its mirror image. If the two substituents on either end of the allene are the same, as in 1,2-propadiene, then there will be only a single optically inactive compound.

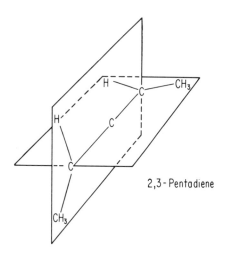

2,3-Pentadiene

These optically active allenes show their optical activity for a reason slightly different from any of the cases previously discussed. A molecule such as 3-methylhexane is optically active because of an asymmetric carbon. In 2,3-pentadiene there is no asymmetric atom, but rather the molecule as a whole is asymmetric. In predicting whether or not a molecule is capable of having optical isomers, the test mentioned earlier was to note whether or not at least one of the carbons has four different substituents attached to it; if it does, there exist optical isomers. This is a good working rule, which covers about 99% of the known cases. There are a few cases known, however, such as the allenes, that it does not cover. When there is any question, the absolute test which works in 100% of the cases is: can the *molecule* be superimposed on its mirror image? If it cannot, it will exist as a pair of enantiomers; if it can, it is a single optically inactive compound.

An allene represents the simplest case of a *cumulated* system of double bonds, just as 1,3-butadiene represents the simplest case of conjugated double bonds. Large numbers of more complicated systems of both kinds are known. The group CH$_2$=CH— is called a vinyl group, and compounds which differ by the addition of a —CH=CH— group are called *vinylogs.* The next higher vinylog of 1,3-butadiene is 1,3,5-hexatriene (CH$_2$=CH—CH=CH—CH=CH$_2$), and many higher and more complicated vinylogs are known. An example of a polyene that occurs naturally, and also is interesting in other ways, is vitamin A.

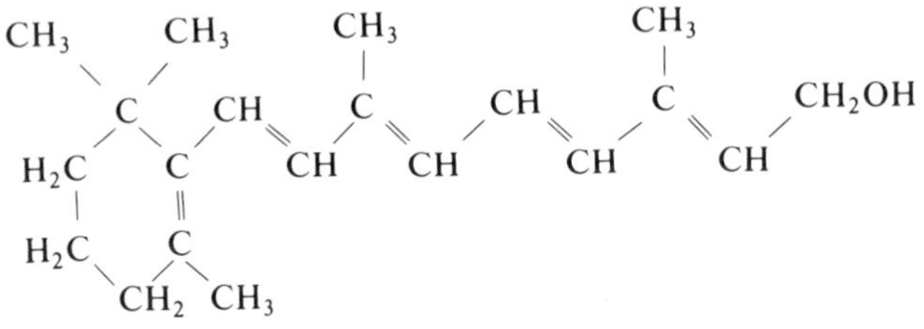

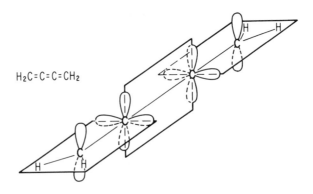

vitamin A

The isomer problem with such molecules is straightforward. Two substituents may be either *cis* or *trans* across each double bond (except in the ring, where only the *cis* type is physically possible). The *s-cis* and *s-trans* isomers do not correspond to isolable species; hence there are 2^4, or 16, possible geometrical isomers (optically inactive) of the structure shown. Only one of these isomers is vitamin A (it happens to be the all-*trans* one); the synthetic chemist is usually interested in preparing a single isomer from among those possible, and this can at times constitute an exceedingly difficult practical problem.

The isomer problem with the cumulenes is more involved than with the conjugated polyenes. The general principles are best understood by looking at the next member of the series, 1,2,3-butatriene. Here the three components of the double bonds lie in alternating planes, and *cis-trans*

$$H_2C=C=C=CH_2$$

isomers rather than optical isomers are possible. Hence, for the substituted cumulenes containing an odd number of double bonds (including substituted derivatives of ethylene and of 1,2,3-butatriene) there exists the possibility of *cis-trans* isomers. If the cumulene contains an even number of double bonds (as do the allenes), then there will instead exist optical isomers.

Conjugation of two double bonds in general causes each of their stretching motions to yield lower frequencies in the infrared. The reason for the shift is best seen from the valence bond resonance forms shown earlier. This resonance reduces the double-bond character of the olefin and makes it a little more like a single bond. The bond is therefore weaker, and hence would be expected to have a lower stretching frequency, and this is what is found experimentally. An ordinary olefin absorbs near 1650 cm^{-1}, whereas the conjugated diene absorbs near 1600 cm^{-1}.

4.4 ALICYCLIC HYDROCARBONS

The alkanes and unsaturated hydrocarbons we have so far discussed have for the most part been open-chain compounds that do not contain rings. Such compounds belong to the general group of *acyclic* hydrocarbons. There is another group of hydrocarbons in which cyclic systems are present; vitamin A is one such. These are the aliphatic cyclic, or *alicyclic* compounds.

The cyclic hydrocarbons have the same formulas as do the alkenes, $C_n H_{2n}$. In a formal sense, the smallest stable member of the series is ethylene, which can be considered a two-membered ring. The olefins have completely different chemical properties from those of the higher cycloalkanes, however, and the three-membered ring compound, cyclopropane, is usually considered to be the smallest homologue of this series; the higher members are cyclobutane, cyclopentane, cyclohexane, and so on.

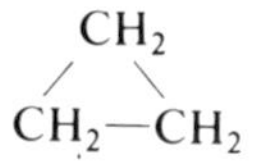

cyclopropane 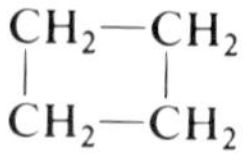   cyclobutane 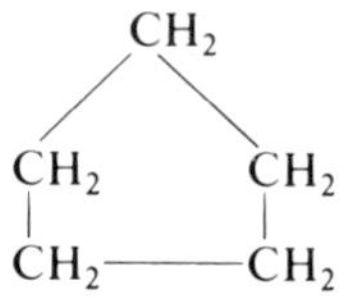   cyclopentane 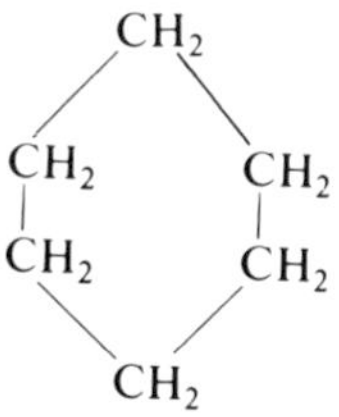   cyclohexane

Cyclopentane and cyclohexane are similar to the acyclic alkanes in almost all of their physical and chemical properties; the smaller rings, however, have properties more different. The reason for the unusual behavior of the small rings lies in the fact that a saturated (sp^3) carbon tends to have bond angles near the tetrahedral value (109½°) and the geometric requirements of the small rings reduce these angles to much smaller values. It is found that the orbitals of carbon which are formed by hybridization can have interorbital angles in the range of 90 to 180°, corresponding to 0 to 50% s character. There is no hybrid combination of s and p orbitals which will yield an interorbital angle of less than 90°. This means that in cyclopropane the carbons do not have their bonding orbitals directed at one another, and the C—C σ bonds are best described as "bent."

While the C—C—C interorbital angeles in cyclobutane could be 90°, the resulting bonds would be pure p and very weak. It is found

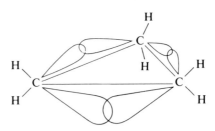

that the addition of some s character makes them stronger, even though they are not collinear. Cyclobutane, and especially cyclopropane, are said to have bent bonds, and while these molecules are stable in the sense that they exist, they are highly strained. A chemical reaction that leads to the rupture of a strained ring releases this strain, and tends to be much more exothermic and to proceed more readily than the same reaction involving a cyclohexane ring or an acyclic system.

Strain in a molecule can be most easily detected from data on its heat of combustion, which are obtained by burning the compound in a calorimeter and measuring the heat evolved. The reaction for an alkane is:

$$C_n H_{2n+2} + \frac{3n+1}{2} O_2 \longrightarrow nCO_2 + (n+1) H_2O + \text{heat}$$

The reason for the usefulness of such data is that the bond between two atoms, say a C—H bond, has an energy which is to a first approximation independent of the nature of the rest of the molecule. The heat of combustion of n-pentane is 845.2 kcal/mole, and that of n-hexane is 1002.6 kcal/mole. The heat of combustion of a single methylene group, then, is 157.4 kcal/mole. Cyclohexane is free of strain, and its heat of combustion might be predicted to be 6 × 157.4 = 944.4 kcal/mole, which is exactly what is found. Cyclopropane, on the other hand, is found to have a heat of combustion of 499.8 kcal/mole, instead of the 472.2 kcal/mole of an unstrained structure. The energy of cyclopropane is, therefore, 27.6 kcal/mole higher than that of an unstrained structure. Rings larger than cyclohexane are quite stable, but they present a special group of properties which will be considered in Chap. 6.

4.5 AROMATIC HYDROCARBONS

Cyclohexane is a typical hydrocarbon in almost all respects. To save writing, it is often represented simply as a hexagon. Cyclohexene is an ordinary olefin with a *cis* geometry, as the *trans* arrangement cannot be accommodated within the geometric constraints of a six-membered ring. Similarly, 1,3-cyclohexadiene is an ordinary conjugated diene. If there is introduced into the ring a third double bond, the resulting compound is called benzene.

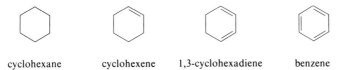

cyclohexane   cyclohexene   1,3-cyclohexadiene   benzene

Benzene has very different properties from those which might have been expected in a polyene. The marked characteristic noted first by the early chemists was the chemical inertness of the compound. Benzene and similar inert cyclic polyenes are referred to as "aromatic" compounds. Alkanes are chemically quite inert whereas alkenes tend to add reagents to the double bond. By adding an H_2 molecule, for example, alkenes can form two very strong C—H σ bonds, at the cost of breaking one strong H—H bond and a weak C—C π bond. Polyenes tend to be even more reactive. Benzene, on the other hand, is scarcely more reactive than an alkane.

The inertness of benzene goes hand in hand with its stability. If benzene is burned, it is found that the amount of heat obtained is much less than one might have anticipated from the number and kinds of bonds in the molecule. The fact that the amount of heat evolved is small means that the heat or energy content of the molecule is small; that is, the compound is very stable. A real understanding of this stability is possible only in terms of quantum theory, but Kekulé actually had the right idea a century ago. Kekulé noted that there are two ways one can write benzene, which correspond to putting a double bond either between atoms 1 and 2 or between atoms 2 and 3:

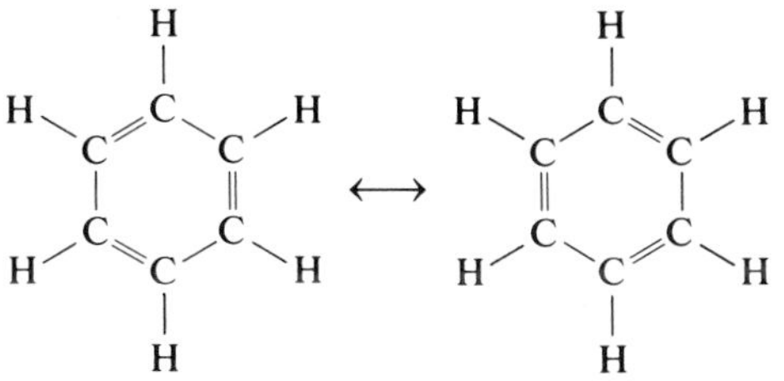

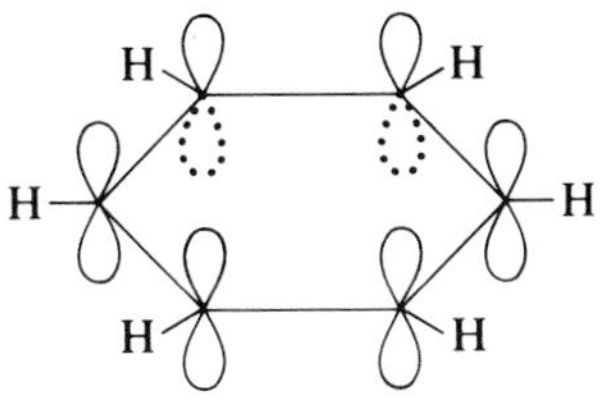

The two different structures are today called resonance forms or Kekulé forms (Sec. 3.2). They are characterized by the fact that all the atomic nuclei have the same positions in the two forms but the electrons have been moved. Whereas in a simple or conjugated alkene there is only one principal resonance form (the others involve charge separation), in benzene there are two equally favorable resonance forms. The two Kekulé forms really tell us that the π electrons are delocalized all around the ring, instead of being confined to specific pairs of carbons, and from the Schrödinger equation it is found that, in general, if the potential field is maintained constant, the larger the volume of space in which an electron is confined, the lower its energy can be. The orbital picture shows that the C—C—C bond angles expected for benzene are 120° (sp^2), the angles of a regular hexagon. The $2p$ orbitals which combine to make the π molecular orbitals are all equivalent, and this suggests the same equivalency as have the two Kekulé forms taken together.

Benzene has always been an important molecule from a theoretical point of view. It contains 12 nuclei and 42 electrons, and even a very crude approximate solution of the Schrödinger equation for such a system is formidable indeed. Most of the properties of interest in benzene may be attributed to the π system. Since this system is orthogonal to the σ system, it is possible to separate mathematically the π system from the rest of the molecule and to study it independently. Thus, to obtain a solution adequate for many purposes one needs to consider only the six π electrons moving in the potential field of the rest of the system, which reduces the problem to the point where a pretty good approximation to the accurate solution of the Schrödinger equation is possible. Some of the results of such solutions for ethylene and benzene are as follows, considering only the π systems in a simplified manner. If we have two carbon atoms, on each of which there is a p orbital containing one electron, we can let the carbons come together and form π bonding and antibonding orbitals. The bonding orbital contains two electrons and has an energy we will call 2β (one β for each electron), as indicated in Fig. 4-3 (β, which is called the resonance integral, is a negative number, so larger numbers of β correspond to lower energies). The system is formally similar to the H_2 molecule, and the bonding (π) and antibonding (π*) orbitals have wave

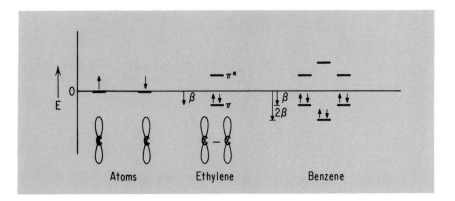

Fig. 4-3 The orbital energies of the π systems in ethylene and benzene.

functions $\psi_\pi = \psi_1 + \psi_2$ and $\psi_{\pi*} = \psi_1 - \psi_2$ respectively, analogous to those in H_2. If we now allow three ethylenes to come together to form benzene, we find that the orbital energies are as indicated in Fig. 4-3, and the total π energy is thus calculated to be 8β, or 2β more than for the three separate ethylenes. This 2β is called the resonance energy of benzene (meaning beyond that of the separate ethylenes), or the conjugation energy. The conjugation energy of butadiene is very small, so if a chemical reaction occurs which converts this benzene system to a butadiene system, there is required, not 2β of energy as with ethylene, but 4β. Hence the relative inertness of benzene to chemical reactions.

The orbital of lowest energy in benzene is perfectly symmetrical, and can be written $\psi_{\pi_1} = \psi_1 + \psi_2 + \psi_3 + \psi_4 + \psi_5 + \psi_6$. The next two orbitals (ψ_{π_2} and ψ_{π_3}) are degenerate and exhibit certain mathematical peculiarities. These two orbitals taken together give a symmetrical distribution for the four electrons, and they can be individually pictured in various ways, one of which is shown in the accompanying photograph.

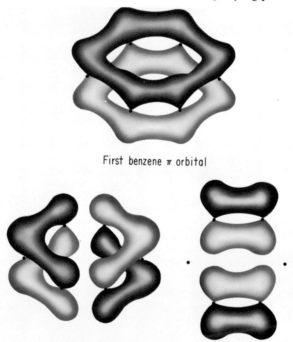

First benzene π orbital

Second and third benzene π orbitals

(From *Organic Chemistry*, Second Edition, by Cram and Hammond. Copyright 1964, McGraw-Hill Book Company. Used by permission.)

As the discussion above implies, in benzene the carbon-carbon bond lengths are all equal (1.39 Å), which length is between that found for ordinary double bonds (1.33 Å) and that of single bonds (1.54 Å).

When a benzene ring is a substituent on another molecule, the substituent is called phenyl. Thus, two benzene rings joined together form biphenyl, and a cyclohexane joined to a benzene may be called phenylcyclohexane or cyclohexylbenzene.

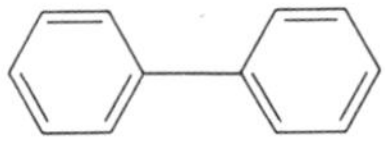

biphenyl 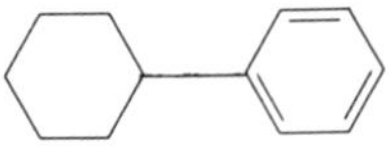   cyclohexylbenzene

Biphenyl is similar to benzene in most respects. There are other aromatic hydrocarbons which differ significantly in their properties from benzene, and these are the fused-ring systems, of which examples are:

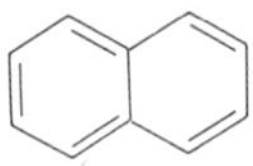

napthalene 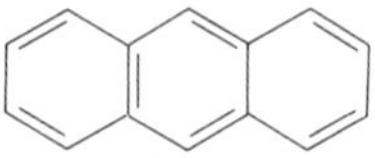   anthracene 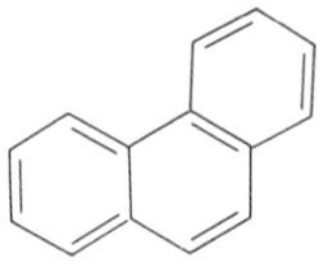   phenanthrene

The principal difference between these systems and benzene is the greater chemical reactivity of the former. This difference can be qualitatively understood in terms of Kekulé forms. Anthracene, for example, has four Kekulé forms. It can be seen that, if something is added across the center ring to give the structure shown below, the new structure still has four Kekulé forms:

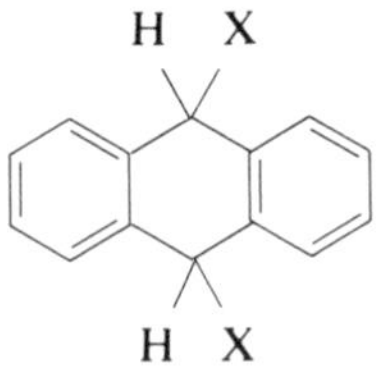

H X   H X

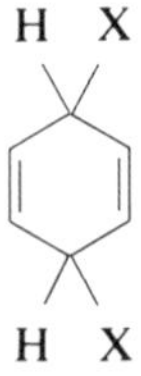

H X   H X

In benzene itself such an addition destroys the stable aromatic system, leads to a single Kekulé form, and thus is energetically unfavorable. In anthracene, the addition modifies but does not destroy the aromatic system and, as a result, anthracene is almost olefinic in many of its chemical properties.

The lower and higher vinylogs of benzene, cyclobutadiene and cyclooctatetraene respectively, have long been of interest to chemists:

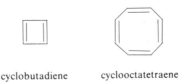

cyclobutadiene   cyclooctatetraene

Cyclobutadiene has never been isolated, in spite of the innumerable attempts made. Although two Kekulé forms for the molecule can be written, quantitative calculations indicate that the molecule should have little or no resonance energy, and the difficulty of synthesis is consistent with this prediction. Cyclooctatetraene is predicted to have a rather small conjugation energy in the planar form. In this form the carbon-carbon bond angles must expand to 135°, and such an expansion would introduce considerable strain into the σ bond system. Alternatively, the molecule might adopt a tub shape, which would have an almost negligible resonance energy but could have natural (120°) bond angles. Detailed calculations have shown the latter to be the energetically favored arrangement, and electron diffraction studies have shown that this is the way the molecule actually exists. It is essentially a polyene with alternating double and single bonds, and it lacks the aromatic properties of benzene.

The approximate solutions of the Schrödinger equation for the π systems of the cyclic planar polyenes show that the orbital energies follow a definite pattern. In each case there is a single orbital of lowest energy, the remaining orbitals always come in degenerate pairs (as in benzene, Fig. 4-3 and, finally, there is a single π* orbital of highest energy. The

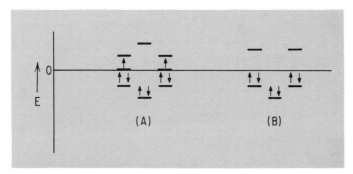

Fig. 4-4 Orbital energies for the systems of (planar) cyclooctatetraene (A) and cyclopentadienide ion (B).

mathematical solution is similar if the number of orbitals is odd (Fig. 4-4), although such a system, of course, corresponds to a radical rather than a polyene and the highest energy level is degenerate. For benzene there are six π electrons, which lead to a filled shell. In cyclooctatetraene there are eight, which do not lead to a filled shell. The half-filled shell can be completed by the addition of two more electrons, and experimentally it was found that cyclooctatetraene reacts with two moles of lithium to form Li_2 (Cot), in which the cyclooctatetraene dianion is present. Inspection of the energy levels for such systems shows that a filled shell will result if there are $2 + 4n$ π electrons; two are required to fill the lowest level while four are required for each succeeding level. Hückel's Rule states that $2 + 4n$ π electrons (as in benzene) lead to an aromatic system, while other numbers of π electrons (as in cyclooctatraene or cyclobutadiene) do not. Thus there are a number of closed-shell π systems containing 2, 6, 10, $\cdots$, etc., electrons, and they have a considerable stability for reasons which are quite analogous to those that confer the "rare gas" stability on atoms containing specified numbers of electrons.

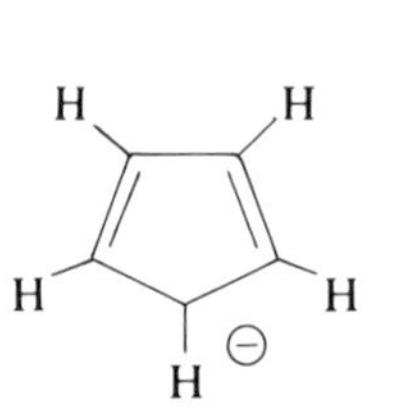

The formation of an aromatic system is energetically very favorable, and Hückel's rule has been useful in predicting a number of interesting facts. Cyclopentadiene, for example, reacts with potassium metal to form the relatively stable cyclopentadienide ion, but the corresponding cation is unstable. In the corresponding cycloheptatriene system the tropylium cation is stable, the anion is not. These facts are nicely predicted by Hückel's Rule.

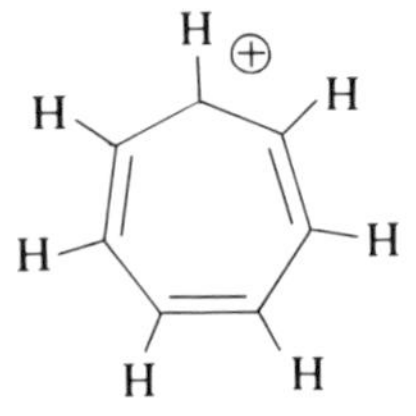

cyclopentadienide ion   tropylium ion

One other aromatic compound which deserves mention is azulene. Its most conspicuous property is its intense blue color. It contains fused five- and seven-membered rings, and it is an isomer of naphthalene. It is somewhat strained because of the unnatural bond angles, but is properly considered an aromatic system:

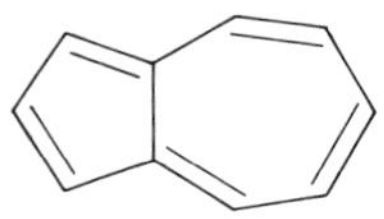

azulene

The infrared spectra of aromatic hydrocarbons show C—H and C=C stretching frequencies similar to those shown by conjugated olefins. The hydrogens on a benzene ring all couple together and show strong out-of-plane bending in the 700 to 1000 cm^{-1} region. The infrared spectra of benzene derivatives can thus be used to establish the arrangements of substituents on the aromatic ring in the same way that the corresponding portion of the spectra can be used to establish substitution patterns in olefins.

The protons on alkyl groups show NMR peaks in the vicinity of 8 to 9 τ. If the electrons in the C—H bond are pushed more toward the proton, the proton is said to be more shielded by the excess electron density, and the peaks are at higher values of τ. As discussed in Sec. 4.2, the electrons in the vinyl C—H bond in an olefin are pulled in closer to carbon, and hence away from the proton. The latter is therefore deshielded, and shows resonance in the 4 to 6 τ region. The protons on the methyls of cis-2-butene (Fig. 4-5) are also more deshielded than is a methyl in an alkane, but the effect is smaller on methyl protons than on vinyl protons. The sp^2

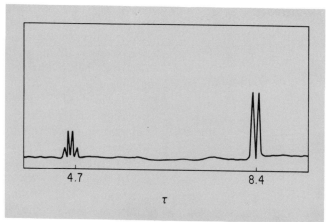

Fig. 4-5 The NMR spectrum of cis-2-butene. Note that the vinylic hydrogens are equivalent and do not couple with one another.

carbon pulls the electrons from the CH_3—C bond toward itself, leaving the methyl carbon a little more positive, and the latter responds by pulling the electrons from the C—H bonds in toward itself a little more. This transmission of an electrical imbalance down a chain is referred to as the *inductive effect.* The effect falls off rapidly with distance, but may sometimes be detected at a point several atoms removed from the disturbance.

The aromatic rings have their attached hydrogens shifted to even lower fields in the NMR spectrum than do the vinyl groups. This is because in the aromatic system the applied magnetic field induces a flow of electrons around the ring, and these flowing electrons generate a magnetic field of their own, which affects the total magnetic field felt by the aromatic proton. Thus, benzene shows a single absorption line from its six equivalent protons at 2.7 τ.

4.6 ULTRAVIOLET SPECTRA

These spectra result from the transitions of electrons from one orbital to another, and are recorded in the wavelength region of about 100 to 700 mμ (one mμ is 10^{-6} mm, or 10 Å).[†] The region below about 180 mμ is

[†]The visible portion of the spectrum (from about 400 to 700 mμ) is thus usually counted as a portion of the ultraviolet, since the same types of transitions (electronic) are observed in both.

difficult to observe experimentally, because oxygen molecules absorb in this region and air is therefore opaque to such radiation. Measurements can be made in vacuum, but this is difficult and therefore the region above 180 mμ in the spectra of most molecules has been the more thoroughly studied.

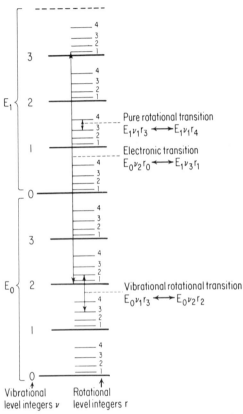

Pure rotational transition
$E_1\nu_1r_3 \longleftrightarrow E_1\nu_1r_4$

Electronic transition
$E_0\nu_2r_0 \longleftrightarrow E_1\nu_3r_1$

Vibrational rotational transition
$E_0\nu_1r_3 \longleftrightarrow E_0\nu_2r_2$

Vibrational level integers ν Rotational level integers r

Fig. 4-6 Schematic of the spectroscopic states of a simple molecule.

A hydrogen atom shows a well-known series of spectral lines in the ultraviolet region. Absorption spectra are a result of the electron's being excited (that is, moving from one atomic orbital to another of higher energy). Emission spectra are a result of its falling from one orbital to another of lower energy. Excitations of electrons to higher atomic orbitals are found also in such molecules as ethane. The carbon $1s$ electrons can, for example, be excited to the 3 or 4 quantum level. There are some additional features in molecular spectra which are of greater interest, however. In ethane, for example, there are bonding orbitals (one for each pair of atoms joined together), and an equal number of antibonding orbitals. It is thus possible, with varying degrees of probability, for an electron in any of the bonding orbitals to be excited to any of the antibonding orbitals; such transitions are called $\sigma \longrightarrow \sigma*$ transitions[†] (they are summarized in Fig. 4-6). It is also possible for nonbonding electrons (like the carbon $1s$) to be excited to the $\sigma*$ orbitals and also for bonding electrons to be excited to higher, empty, atomic orbitals. The ultraviolet spectrum of ethane is, consequently, very complicated, and nearly all the transitions occur in the relatively inaccessible part of the spectrum below 180 mμ. The other alkanes have ultraviolet spectra which are in general similar to

[†]Vibrational and rotational transitions of varying types accompany the electronic transitions, and the former correspond to small energy changes superimposed on the latter. An electronic transition doesn't give a single line in the spectrum, therefore, but a series of closely spaced lines or a band.

that of ethane. Because of both theoretical complexities and experimental difficulties, however, the spectra of the alkanes have not been studied in much detail.

The spectra of olefins have been a little more revealing. The π bond in ethylene is much weaker than an ordinary σ bond, and this means that the π (bonding) orbital does not have as low an energy, nor does the π^* (antibonding) orbital have as high an energy, as do their σ and σ^* counterparts in ethane (Fig. 4-7). There is in ethylene and in simple olefins a $\pi \longrightarrow \pi^*$ transition which usually occurs in the 170 to 190 mμ region.

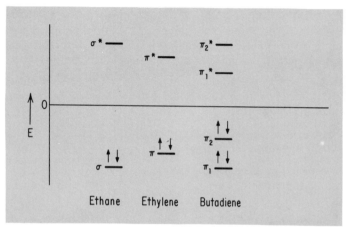

Fig. 4-7 Some electronic energy levels of simple molecules.

This particular band in the absorption spectrum is very intense and can usually be recognized if present. Such an absorption is most useful in conjugated systems. In butadiene, for example, there are two π orbitals, containing a total of four electrons, and two empty π^* orbitals. The relative energies of these orbitals are as indicated in Fig. 4-7. If there were two ethylenes far removed from one another, the two molecules together would have two π orbitals of the same energy and two π^* orbitals of the same energy. Solution of the Schrödinger equation (by approximate methods) shows that, just as the two identical atomic levels of the hydrogen atoms split apart (one increasing, the other decreasing, in energy) to give σ and σ^* orbitals as the atoms come close together, so do the π and π^* orbitals in the two ethylenes split apart. This means that in butadiene there is a relatively small energy difference between the highest π and lowest π^* orbital, and the corresponding transition is at a relatively long wavelength, near 215 mμ. Other olefins containing more than two conjugated double bonds show absorption at even longer wavelengths. It has been found that the exact position of the absorption depends on, among other things, the exact number of alkyl groups attached to the olefinic carbons, and it is also a function of the degree of planarity of the system.[†] Ultraviolet spectra have so far proven to be of little use in the study of saturated organic molecules, but they have been extremely informative with respect to unsaturated, and especially conjugated, systems.

4.7 PROBLEMS

1. Draw orbital pictures of the following molecules, indicating the hybridization of each orbital, the bond angles, and the π and σ bonds: (a) ethylene (b) acetylene, (c) ethane, (d) allene, (e) benzene.

2. (a) Predict where strong absorption bands will be found in the infrared region for *cis*-2-butene, and the motion assigned to each. (b) What differences would be predicted between this spectrum and that of the *trans* isomer?

3. Arrange in order of increasing acidity: $CH_3C\equiv CH$, $H_2C=CH_2$, CH_3CH_3. Explain. $CH_3—CH=CH_2$ is more acidic than ethylene, the most acidic hydrogens being on the methyl. Explain.

4. Write the resonance forms of (a) ethylene, (b) 1,3-butadiene (there are seven principal ones), and (c) 1,3,5-hexatriene.

5. How many geometric isomers are there of 2-methyl-2,4,6-heptatriene? Of 2-methyl-2,4,5-heptatriene?

6. Kerosene (which is a mixture of hydrocarbons, n-$C_{14}H_{30}$ on the average) and liquid oxygen have recently been used as fuel for large spacecraft. If 157.4 kcal/mole of heat is generated per $—CH_2—$ group and 186 kcal/mole per $CH_3—$, how much heat would be generated by burning 1000 kg (about a ton) of kerosene? How much oxygen would be required?

SUGGESTED READINGS

The reader interested in the chemical properties of the unsaturated compounds discussed in this chapter may wish to read another book in the present series, O. L. Chapman, *Functional Groups in Organic Chemistry*, Englewood Cliffs, N.J., Prentice-Hall, 1966 (*in production*). D. Ginsburg, ed., *Non-Benzenoid Aromatic Compounds*, New York, Wiley, 1959, covers in detail the title subject with respect to both structure and reactivity. Further information on ultraviolet spectra may be found in J. R. Dyer, *Applications of Absorption Spectroscopy of Organic Compounds*, Englewood Cliffs, N.J., Prentice-Hall, 1965.

[†]If the two ethylenic linkages in butadiene lie in planes at right angles to one another, the central bond has a bond order of only 1. The two ethylenic systems do not interact, and the spectrum is essentially that of two separate molecules of ethylene. The splitting apart of the two π levels depends approximately on the square of the cosine of the angle between the olefinic planes.

5

Functionally Substituted Compounds

Most organic molecules contain carbon, hydrogen, and one or more additional elements. One or more atoms of oxygen, nitrogen, sulfur, halogen, or other elements are usually present, and oxygen is the most commonly encountered. These *heteroatoms* are, depending on the molecule, either singly or multiply bonded to the other elements, usually to carbon.

5.1 LEWIS ACIDS AND LEWIS BASES

The covalent bonds we have discussed so far are formed by the combining of two atoms in such a way that each atom furnishes one of the electrons necessary for bond formation: for example, $2H\cdot \longrightarrow H-H$. There is another way in which a covalent bond may be formed, and that is if one atom supplies two electrons and the other supplies none; for example,

$$H:\overset{\overset{\displaystyle H}{\cdot\cdot}}{\underset{\displaystyle H}{N}}: \;+\; \overset{\oplus}{H} \longrightarrow H:\overset{\overset{\displaystyle H}{\cdot\cdot}}{\underset{\displaystyle H}{N}}:H \;\overset{\oplus}{}$$

Such a reaction is an acid-base reaction. In an acid-base reaction, a covalent bond is formed between two atoms, the base supplying both electrons and hence changing its *formal charge* by +1.[†] The older definitions were that an acid is a compound which furnishes protons and a base is anything that reacts with these protons. Lewis pointed out that there are many compounds which do not contain hydrogen but which behave as

---

[†] The formal charge on an atom is found by counting the number of electrons about the atom which are unshared and adding to this number one half of the electrons the atom is sharing by covalent bond formation (since, in a formal sense, a covalent bond can be thought of as containing one electron from each bonded atom). If this number is the same as the number of electrons in the neutral isolated atom, the formal charge is zero; if it is greater by 1 or 2 or 3, etc., then the formal charge is -1 or -2 or -3, etc., respectively. If the number is smaller by 1 or 2 or 3, the formal charge is $+1$, $+2$, $+3$. Thus, $H^{\oplus}$ has a formal charge of $+1$, as does the nitrogen atom in the ammonium ion. The hydrogens in the ammonium ion have formal charges of zero.

acids in that they will accept a pair of electrons in covalent bond formation. Such compounds, as well as those containing hydrogen, are now
referred to as *Lewis acids*. *Lewis bases* are compounds which will donate
an electron pair in covalent bond formation. Lewis acids and bases, then,
include ordinary acids and bases as special cases, and the reaction NH_3 +
$H^{\oplus} \longrightarrow NH_4^{\oplus}$ can therefore be described as the reaction of a Lewis base
with a Lewis acid.

The elements to the left and right of carbon in the periodic table form
respectively Lewis acids and bases in most of their compounds, and they
form salts with each other. Trimethylboron, for example, reacts with dimethyl ether or ammonia to form addition compounds, as shown:

$$
\begin{array}{c}
\text{CH}_3 \\ | \\
\text{CH}_3\!-\!\text{B} \\ | \\ \text{CH}_3
\end{array}
\quad + \quad
\begin{array}{c}
\text{CH}_3 \\ | \\ :\!\text{O}\!-\!\text{CH}_3
\end{array}
\quad \longrightarrow \quad
\begin{array}{c}
\text{CH}_3 \quad \text{CH}_3 \\ | \qquad | \\ \text{CH}_3\!\overset{\ominus}{-}\!\text{B}\!-\!\!-\!\overset{\oplus}{\text{O}}: \\ | \qquad | \\ \text{CH}_3 \quad \text{CH}_3
\end{array}
$$

$$
\begin{array}{c}
\text{CH}_3 \\ | \\ \text{CH}_3\!-\!\text{B} \\ | \\ \text{CH}_3
\end{array}
\quad + \quad
\begin{array}{c}
\text{H} \\ | \\ :\!\text{NH} \\ | \\ \text{H}
\end{array}
\quad \longrightarrow \quad
\begin{array}{c}
\text{CH}_3 \quad \text{H} \\ | \qquad | \\ \text{CH}_3\!\overset{\ominus}{-}\!\text{B}\!-\!\!-\!\overset{\oplus}{\text{N}}\!-\!\text{H} \\ | \qquad | \\ \text{CH}_3 \quad \text{H}
\end{array}
$$

5.2 SINGLY BONDED SUBSTITUENTS CONTAINING
ELECTROPOSITIVE ELEMENTS

All of the elements in the first row of the periodic table, except neon,
are found as constituents in organic molecules, and we wish to examine
the properties of each of them. The hybridization of carbon has been previously discussed in some detail, and we now consider the hybridization
that may be expected in these other electropositive elements. The rules
to be used for predicting geometry and hybridization, in their order of
importance, are:

1. use the $2s$ orbital as efficiently as possible.
2. form bonds which are as strong as possible.
3. place the atomic nuclei as far apart as possible, consistent with bond
length.

Rule 1, in the limiting case, follows from the fact that an electron will
have a lower energy in an s orbital than in a p orbital. In methane, the
four electrons formally belonging to carbon were each in an sp^3 orbital,
so each had $\frac{1}{4}s$ character. We can, therefore, say that 4 electrons $\times \frac{1}{4}s$
character = $1s$ (the equivalent of one electron). Since the s orbital will
hold 2 electrons, we have utilized $\frac{1}{2}$ of the $2s$ orbital, which is the best
that can be done for methane. The bond strengths vary in the order
$sp^3 > p > s$ (with sp and sp^2 similar to sp^3), so methane satisfies rule 2,
and the tetrahedral arrangement allows rule 3 to be satisfied. Thus, for

methane sp^3 hybridization and a tetrahedral geometry are predicted unambiguously.

Various lithium derivatives of hydrocarbons, such as lithium methide and lithium ethide, are known. The first of these has the formula $LiCH_3$ and is an arrangement in which one of the hydrogens in methane has been replaced by lithium. Actually, methane is too weak an acid to react with lithium directly, but the compound can be prepared by more roundabout methods. The lithium-carbon bond can be written as a covalent bond, but we would expect a large contribution from the ionic form, as shown below, because of the electropositive character of the lithium:

$$H_3C\text{:}Li \longleftrightarrow H_3\overset{\ominus}{C}\text{:} + \overset{\oplus}{Li}$$

The bond is, in fact, covalent, but highly polar. It is easy to get the lithium to ionize away from carbon in chemical reactions, but in the isolated molecule the covalent structure is stable.

Lithium has a single $2s$ electron which may be used for bond formation. The criterion given by rule 1 then requires that the lithium use this $2s$ orbital for bonding, since the orbital is thereby one-half utilized. If the lithium orbital used for bonding were to be, say, sp, then only one quarter of the s orbital would be used. This would allow for a stronger bond, but the gain in bond strength would not be sufficient to outweigh the inefficient utilization of the s orbital (rule 1 is more important than rule 2), and the best arrangement is the use by lithium of a $2s$ orbital for bonding.[†] The $2p$ orbitals of lithium are empty, and empty orbitals always tend to be p, as a consequence of rule 1.

The next element, beryllium, is divalent and forms organic derivatives such as dimethylberyllium:

$$CH_3\text{---}Be\text{---}CH_3 \longleftrightarrow CH_3\text{---}\overset{\oplus}{Be} \;\text{:}\overset{\ominus}{C}H_3 \longleftrightarrow \overset{\ominus}{C}H_3\text{:} \;\overset{\oplus\oplus}{Be} \;\text{:}\overset{\ominus}{C}H_3$$

Beryllium in such a compound lacks a filled shell and is not very stable. To attain a filled shell, the doubly ionized species is required. The double ionization is unfavorable with such a small atom, and consequently the ionic resonance forms contribute to the hybrid less than in the case of lithium methide. The application of the hybridization rules to beryllium leads unambiguously to the following conclusions. Dimethylberyllium has sp orbitals on beryllium overlapping with sp^3 orbitals on carbon. The sp orbitals are directed 180° from one another, so the C—Be—C system is linear. There are two empty $2p$ orbitals on beryllium which are perpendicular to the C—Be—C axis and to each other. The s orbital on beryllium therefore is used as fully as possible in bond formation.

[†] This is an approximate statement. In all such cases a compromise is reached in practice. Here the addition of a few percent of p character to the bonding orbital strengthens the bond sufficiently to outweigh the small decrease in the utilization of the s orbital, and this is the hybridization which actually exists in Li_2.

Dicovalent beryllium is a Lewis acid and it will react with a Lewis base, such as lithium methide, to form a compound in which the carbon of the methide is covalently bound to beryllium. The latter then carries a formal negative charge, and the resulting trimethylberyllium anion is associated with the positive lithium ion:

$$Li—CH_3 + CH_3—Be—CH_3 \longrightarrow CH_3—\overset{\ominus}{\underset{\underset{CH_3}{|}}{Be}}—CH_3 + Li^{\oplus}$$

In this salt the beryllium atom is sp^2 hybridized, similar to a carbon in ethylene. The three methyls are equivalent to one another, in one plane, and 120° apart. Again, a $2p$ orbital is left vacant.

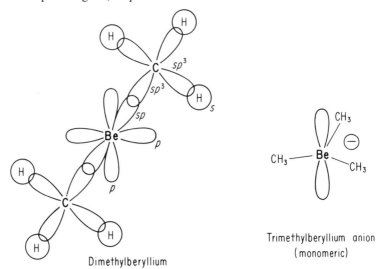

Dimethylberyllium

Trimethylberyllium anion
(monomeric)

Continuing across the periodic table, boron is trivalent and forms compounds, such as trimethylboron, in which the boron is two electrons short of having a complete octet. These compounds, then, are Lewis acids. Such a boron atom exists preferentially in a trigonal planar arrangement having C—B—C angles at 120° and an empty $2p$ orbital. The chemistry of boron is complicated and interesting, but somewhat outside the scope of the present considerations; we can note, however, that a compound lithium borohydride exists, in which there is a lithium cation and a $BH_4^{\ominus}$ anion. The latter has the tetrahedral geometry of methane and, in principle, comes from the addition of a hydride ion ($H^{\ominus}$) to BH_3.

5.3 SINGLY BONDED SUBSTITUENTS CONTAINING ELECTRONEGATIVE ELEMENTS

Organic compounds containing first-row elements which are to the right of carbon in the periodic table are more common and more important than those previously discussed. Let us first try to predict what kinds of geometry and hybridization will be found with HF, H_2O, and NH_3, in that order.

We shall start with HF. Using the rules of hybridization, we see that, while the electropositive elements had bonding orbitals that tended to be largely *s* in character and empty orbitals that were largely *p*, the electronegative elements have bonding orbitals that contain one electron (formally) and nonbonding orbitals that contain a pair of electrons. To utilize the *s* orbital efficiently, we want to put a pair of electrons in it. Hence, the fluorine orbital to be used for the formation of the covalent H—F bond should, according to rule 1, be a *p* orbital. Contrary to such an arrangement, a small amount of *s* character would yield a stronger bond. There is a compromise, but rule 1 is the more important, and the fluorine bonding orbital is found to contain *p* and *s* character is the ratio of 3 to 1.

Now, for the water molecule, pure *p* bonding orbitals from oxygen would yield a 90° H—O—H angle. By the inclusion of some *s* character in these orbitals the two bonds can be made stronger and the angle between the orbitals to which the hydrogens are bonded can be widened, which will reduce the repulsion between the two hydrogen nuclei. To reduce the repulsion between the hydrogen nuclei still further, without using an excessive amount of the *s* orbital for bonding, the hydrogens can move still farther

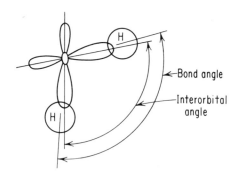

Bonding orbitals of water

apart, off the axes of the oxygen orbitals to which they are bound. The maximum bonding electron density then does not lie directly between the bound atoms, and the bond is bent (Sec. 4.4).

In the water and ammonia molecules the balance of the acting forces is more nearly equal than it is in hydrogen fluoride, and it is found that the bond angles are 105° and 107°, respectively. As far as the geometry is concerned, the ammonia, NH_3, molecule may be looked upon as nearly tetrahedral, with hydrogens at three corners and a lone (unshared) pair at the fourth corner, although the nitrogen orbitals themselves differ somewhat from sp^3 hybridization.

Fluorine forms covalent bonds with many atoms, especially with carbon. Compounds like fluoromethane (CH_3F, also called methyl fluoride) are stable; in fact, they are rather inert typical covalent substances. The C—F bond is formed from the overlap of an sp^3 orbital of carbon with a $2p$ orbital of fluorine. Methyl chloride, methyl bromide, and methyl iodide are likewise typical covalent organic compounds.

Compounds of the type R—X, where R is an alkyl group and X is a halogen, have such trivial names as ethyl bromide and isopropyl iodide.

The IUPAC system of nomenclature is to name the hydrocarbon part of the molecule as usual, and to designate the position of the halogen with the smallest possible number:

CH_3—Br CH_3—$\underset{\underset{Cl}{|}}{CH}$—$CH_3$ CH_3—$\underset{\underset{F}{|}}{CH}$—$CH_2$—$\underset{\underset{CH_3}{|}}{CH}$—$CH_3$

bromomethane   2-chloropropane   2-fluoro-4-methylpentane
(methyl bromide)   (isopropyl chloride)

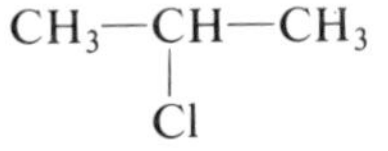

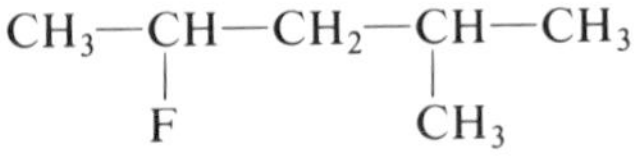

CH_3—$\underset{\underset{I}{|}}{CH}$—$\underset{\underset{H}{|}}{C}$=$\underset{\underset{H}{|}}{C}$—$CH_2$—$CH_3$

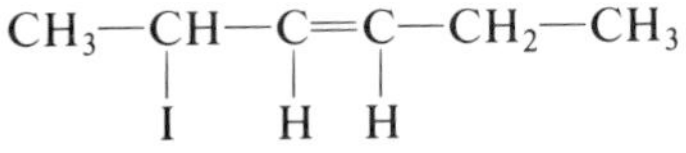

2-iodo-*cis*-3-hexene

We return now to oxygen, the element which, after carbon and hydrogen, is the most commonly found element in organic molecules. Two classes of compounds containing oxygen may be regarded as organic derivatives of water. The first is a series of compounds in which one hydrogen of water has been replaced by an alkyl group. The simplest member of the series is methyl alcohol, or methanol. The next homologue is ethyl alcohol, or ethanol. (The IUPAC system of nomenclature is to replace the final -*e* of the hydrocarbon name by -ol, and to indicate the position of the —OH, hydroxyl, group with the lowest possible number.

CH_3—OH CH_3—CH_2—OH $CH_3CH_2CH_2OH$
methanol   ethanol   1-propanol
                                                (*n*-propyl alcohol)

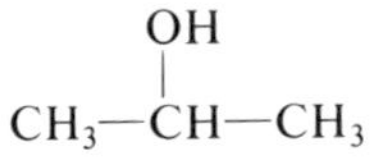

CH_3—$\underset{\underset{}{}}{\overset{\overset{OH}{|}}{CH}}$—$CH_3$ CH_2=CH—CH_2OH
2-propanol   2-propene-1-ol
(isopropyl alcohol)   (allyl alcohol)

It is sometimes convenient to classify alcohols as primary, secondary, or tertiary, according to the number of carbons attached to the carbon carrying the hydroxyl. Thus we have the primary alcohols (1-butanol and 2-methylpropanol), in which only one carbon is so attached, and the secondary and tertiary isomers, in which two and three carbons, respectively, are attached:

CH_3—CH_2—CH_2—CH_2—OH CH_3—$\underset{\underset{CH_3}{|}}{CH}$—$CH_2$—OH

1-butanol   2-methylpropanol
                                       (isobutyl alcohol)

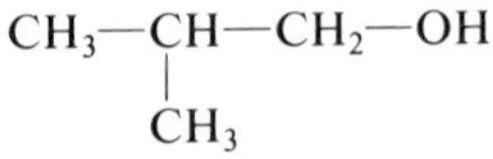

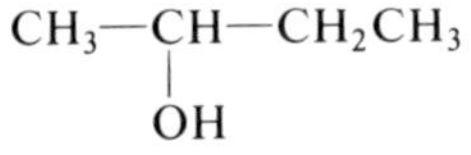

CH_3—$\underset{\underset{OH}{|}}{CH}$—$CH_2CH_3$ CH_3—$\underset{\underset{CH_3}{|}}{\overset{\overset{OH}{|}}{C}}$—$CH_3$

2-butanol   2-methyl-2-propanol
(*sec*-butyl alcohol)   (*tert*-butyl alcohol)

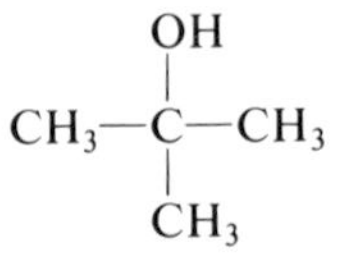

The hybridization of the oxygen atom in an alcohol is the same as in water. Since the oxygen atom is very electronegative, it will support a negative charge rather well, and the hydrogen on the oxygen of an alcohol is therefore weakly acidic, similar to the hydrogen in water.

The second class of organic derivatives of water has both of the hydrogens replaced by alkyl groups to yield compounds called ethers, such as dimethyl ether or methyl ethyl ether:

$$CH_3-O-CH_3 \qquad\qquad CH_3-O-CH_2CH_3$$
dimethyl ether   methyl ethyl ether

Ethers are geometrically similar to water and the alcohols, and do not present any structural considerations of special interest.

There also are compounds in which two oxygens are bound together; these are called peroxides, or hydroperoxides. Like inorganic peroxides, they contain the unstable oxygen-oxygen bond, and hence are powerful oxidizing agents. They are quite unstable compounds, frequently explosive. Two of them are:

$$CH_3-O-O-CH_3 \qquad\qquad CH_3-O-O-H$$
methyl peroxide   methyl hydroperoxide

Compounds that may be looked upon as derivatives of ammonia, just as alcohols and ethers are derivatives of water, are the singly bonded nitrogen derivatives of hydrocarbons, the amines. The nomenclature of the nitrogen compounds is much like that of the alcohols, but the meanings are different. Amines are referred to as primary, secondary, or tertiary, according to the number of alkyl groups attached *to the nitrogen*. Thus methylamine (aminomethane) is a primary amine, as is *tert*-butylamine (2-amino-2-methylpropane), methylethylamine is a secondary amine, and trimethylamine and methylethyl-*sec*-butylamine are tertiary amines:

$$CH_3NH_2 \qquad CH_3-\overset{\displaystyle CH_3}{\underset{\displaystyle CH_3}{C}}-NH_2 \qquad CH_3-\overset{\displaystyle CH_3}{\underset{\displaystyle CH_2CH_3}{N}}-CHCH_2CH_3$$

methylamine   2-amino-2-methylpropane   methylethyl-*sec*-butylamine

$$CH_3-\underset{\displaystyle H}{N}-CH_2CH_3 \qquad\qquad CH_3-\underset{\displaystyle CH_3}{N}-CH_3$$

methylethylamine   trimethylamine

For reasons discussed earlier, the balance between various effects yields a pyramidal geometry for the nitrogen in ammonia derivatives, one close to a tetrahedron, the three substituents and the lone pair occupying the four corners. If the nitrogen were to adopt a planar trigonal geometry, in which the bonding orbitals were sp^2 and the p orbital contained an electron pair, the energy of the molecule would be higher, chiefly because effectively only one electron is in the s orbital $(2 \times 0 + 3 \times \frac{1}{3}$ is the number of electrons formally belonging to nitrogen multiplied by the fraction of s character in each orbital), compared with the $(5 \times \frac{1}{4}) = 1.25$ for sp^3 hybridization. The hydrogen nuclei, however, are farther apart in a trigonal geometry than in a pyramidal one, so that, while the pyramidal geometry is better the difference is not very large compared with the energy of a chemical bond (only about one-tenth as large, in fact). Hence the nitrogen in ammonia or in an amine can invert quite easily, like an umbrella in a windstorm, via the planar configuration. An amine such as

methylethylpropylamine, which is asymmetric at nitrogen (the lone pair acting as the fourth substituent), has never been separated into enantiomers, because the latter interconvert too rapidly at room temperature.

The case of nitrogen may be contrasted with that of carbon. In methane there is a proton attached to what in ammonia is an electron pair. Inversion of the carbon atom therefore requires breaking the C—H bond and then moving the proton around and attaching it to the other side.

Ammonia is a Lewis base and will share its lone pair of electrons with a Lewis acid (for example, a proton) to form a salt; if it shares its electrons with a proton, it forms $NH_4^{\oplus}$. The ammonium ion is geometrically analogous to methane and is a regular tetrahedron. Amines form salts similar to those of ammonia; $CH_3NH_3^{\oplus}Cl^{\ominus}$, for example, is obtained by adding hydrogen chloride to methylamine, and it is called methylammonium chloride. It is an ordinary salt, soluble in water and similar to ammonium chloride. The cation of a quaternary ammonium salt having four different groups attached to nitrogen $(R_1R_2R_3R_4N^{\oplus})$ exists in two enantiomeric forms, as might be supposed. To interconvert them requires, as in the case of the carbon analogue, breaking and remaking a chemical bond.

The infrared spectra of singly bound atoms or groups can often be very informative. The O—H and N—H stretching frequencies are slightly higher than those of C—H and are very useful for identification purposes. The C—O stretching motion leads to an intense absorption in the 1050 to 1150 cm^{-1} range. This is in the fingerprint region, but the band is usually so intense that it may be identified. The C—F absorption occurs near 1000 cm^{-1} and it is often identifiable. The absorptions due to C—N stretching and the bending of the O—H and N—H bonds tend to be weak and to be coupled with other vibrations, and are not very useful. The heavier halogens give absorption in the 500 to 800 cm^{-1} range and are often identifiable, but sometimes the bands are at such low frequency as to be outside a region easily accessible experimentally.

Atoms such as boron or oxygen, which have a nonbonding $2p$ orbital (empty and full, respectively), can conjugate if bound to appropriate systems. The trigonal boron in boric acid, for example, has an empty p orbital and each oxygen has a full one, so resonance can occur:

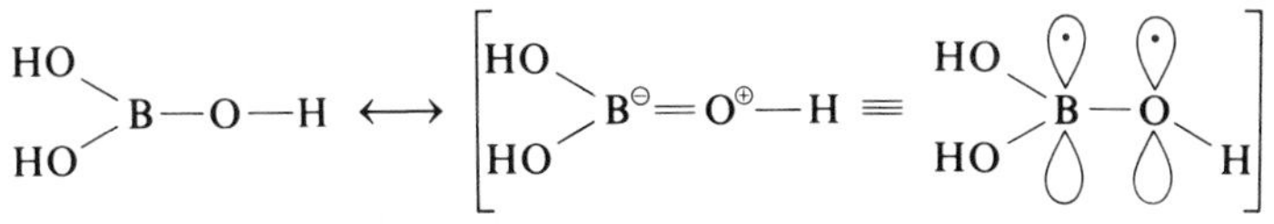

The resonance involves charge separation and is only moderately effective. In the dihydrogen borate ion the resonance is much more effective:

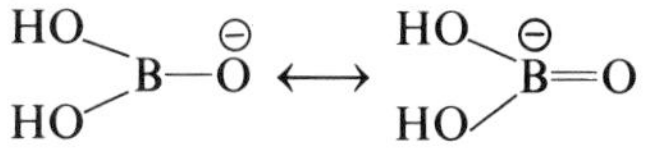

This kind of resonance stabilizes the anion more than the neutral molecule, and shifts the dissociation equilibrium to the right:

$$(HO)_2 B\!-\!OH \longleftrightarrow (HO)_2 B\!-\!O^\ominus + H^\oplus$$

In fact, this is why boric acid is an acid.

If a hydroxyl group is attached to an aromatic ring, a similar effect is noted. Hydroxybenzene is called phenol, and it is an acid because of the resonance stabilization of the anion. The resonance forms of phenol itself, other than the Kekulé forms, involve charge separation. The result is that resonance stabilizes the anion more than the neutral molecule, and it is found that phenol is more acidic than cyclohexanol by about 6 pK units (one million times):

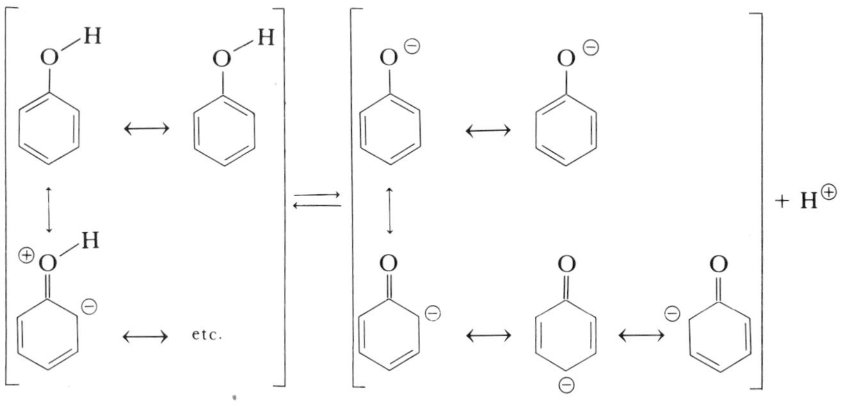

Aminobenzene (aniline) is a compound in which the nonbonding electron pair on nitrogen can resonate with the ring. The resonance forms that result, although they have charge separation, stabilize the molecule to some extent. When the amino group in aniline is protonated, such resonance is no longer possible. The effect of the resonance between the nitrogen and the benzene ring is to stabilize the neutral molecule and to make the compound a weaker base than cyclohexylamine, by a factor of about 10^5:

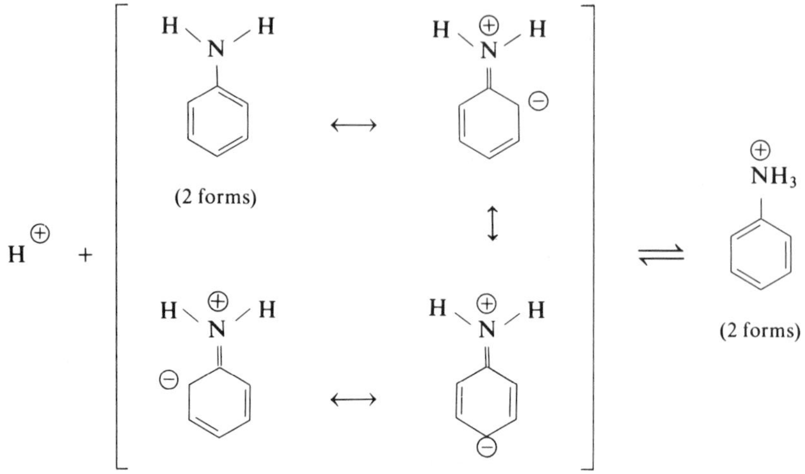

(2 forms)

(2 forms)

The same sort of considerations apply whenever there are two p orbitals on adjacent atoms which are less than completely full. There will be resonance between them, and such is the case in methyl vinyl ether:

$$CH_3-O-CH=CH_2 \longleftrightarrow CH_3-\overset{\oplus}{O}=CH-\overset{\ominus}{C}H_2$$

The compound vinyl alcohol, $CH_2=CHOH$, is a special case. Chemists have tried to prepare this compound by various methods since the last century, but they have never been able to isolate it. They obtained instead a compound called acetaldehyde, $CH_3C\overset{\nearrow O}{\underset{\searrow H}{}}$. Vinyl alcohol and acetaldehyde are said to be *tautomers.*[†] That the compound obtained was acetaldehyde and not vinyl alcohol is best revealed by the NMR spectrum, which shows a doublet with an area of three units and a quartet with an area of one unit. Furthermore, the infrared spectrum shows no band near 3600 cm^{-1} (no O—H) and no band near 1650 cm^{-1} (no C=C), but it does show a strong band at 1730 cm^{-1} which, as we shall see, is characteristic of C=O. The compound exists as the *keto*, $\underset{H}{\overset{|}{C}}-C=O$, rather than as the *enol*, C=C—O—H tautomer, mainly because the C=O bond is so very much stronger than the C=C bond.

Many of the elements in the second row of the periodic table are also

---

[†]Two compounds are said to be tautomers if in one there is a double bond between atoms 1 and 2 and a proton on atom 3, and in the other there is a double bond between atoms 3 and 2 and a proton on atom 1.

moderately common in organic compounds. The bonding in many of the compounds of phosphorus, sulfur, or chlorine is similar to that in the corresponding nitrogen, oxygen, or fluorine analogues. Phosphorus is most often encountered in the form of oxygen derivatives, such as phosphates. Compounds like trimethylphosphine are known, but they are of limited importance. Organic compounds of sulfur are often found with the sulfur in higher oxidation states (Sec. 5.4), but thiols and thioethers analogous to the oxygen compounds are also well known. Thiols are also called mercaptans, and are best noted for their terrible smells.

$$CH_3\!-\!S\!-\!H \qquad CH_3\!-\!S\!-\!CH_3 \qquad CH_3\!-\!S\!-\!S\!-\!CH_3 \qquad CH_3\!-\!\overset{\overset{\displaystyle CH_3}{|}}{\underset{\underset{\displaystyle CH_3}{|}}{S}}{}^{\oplus}Cl^{\ominus}$$

methyl mercaptan   dimethyl thioether   dimethyl disulfide   trimethylsulfonium chloride

The mercaptans are more acidic than the corresponding alcohols, chiefly because the larger sulfur atom can better accommodate the charge of the anion. Sulfur can also better accommodate positive charge, and hence often acts as a better Lewis base than the oxygen analogue. Thus, trimethylsulfonium chloride is a stable salt, but trimethyloxonium chloride is not. Disulfides, formally analogous to peroxides, also exist. The disulfides differ from the peroxides in that they are perfectly stable and ordinary compounds and are, in fact, obtained from mercaptans by oxidation.

5.4 MULTIPLY-BONDED SUBSTITUENTS

The unsaturated hydrocarbons, which we have previously considered (Chap. 4), are the most fundamental group of multiply-bonded compounds. Perhaps the next most fundamental group is comprised of those containing carbon doubly bonded to oxygen. The $\searrow\!C\!=\!O$ group is referred to as the *carbonyl* group. If the carbon is bonded also to one or two hydrogens and not more than one alkyl (or aryl) group, the compounds are called aldehydes. The trivial names are commonly used for such compounds containing up to three or four carbons. The IUPAC names indicate the aldehyde function by replacing the final -e of the hydrocarbon with -al:

formaldehyde (methanal)   acetaldehyde (ethanal)

A closely similar group of compounds, called ketones, have two alkyl (or aryl) groups attached to the carbonyl carbon. Acetone is the simplest ketone. The IUPAC names of the ketones are formed by changing the final -e of the alkane to -one:

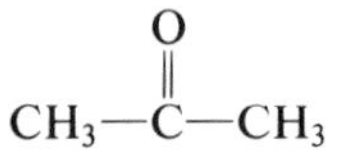

$$CH_3\text{—}\overset{\displaystyle O}{\overset{\|}{C}}\text{—}CH_3 \qquad\qquad CH_3\text{—}\overset{\displaystyle O}{\overset{\|}{C}}\text{—}CH_2CH_3$$

acetone
(propanone)

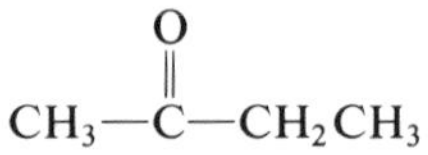

butanone
(methyl ethyl ketone)

The carbonyl carbon is trigonally hybridized, as in an olefin, the C—C—O and C—C—C angles in acetone being close to 120°. The oxygen can be looked upon as essentially unhybridized; the $2p_x$ and $2p_z$ orbitals on oxygen form σ and π bonds, respectively, and the remaining electron pairs on oxygen are in the nonbonding $2p_y$ and $2s$ orbitals. Conjugated ketones, such as methyl vinyl ketone and methyl phenyl ketone are known:

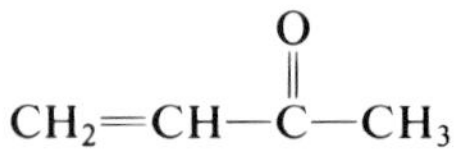

$$CH_2\text{=}CH\text{—}\overset{\displaystyle O}{\overset{\|}{C}}\text{—}CH_3$$

methyl vinyl ketone

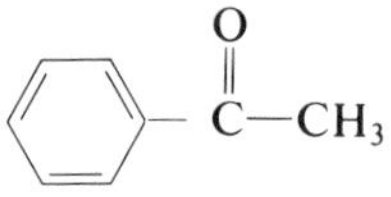

methyl phenyl ketone
(acetophenone)

Their properties are what might be expected from a consideration of butadiene and acetone. There are two principal resonance forms for acetone,

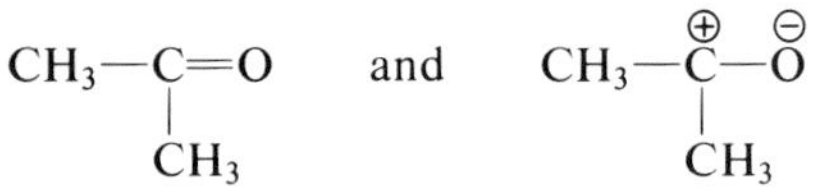

$$CH_3\text{—}\underset{\underset{\displaystyle CH_3}{|}}{C}\text{=}O \qquad \text{and} \qquad CH_3\text{—}\underset{\underset{\displaystyle CH_3}{|}}{\overset{\oplus}{C}}\text{—}\overset{\ominus}{O}$$

For methyl vinyl ketone the form

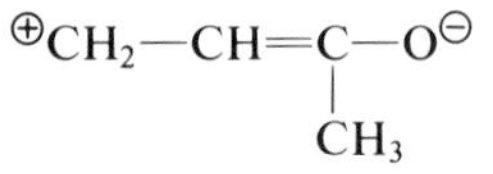

$$\overset{\oplus}{C}H_2\text{—}CH\text{=}\underset{\underset{\displaystyle CH_3}{|}}{C}\text{—}\overset{\ominus}{O}$$

is also important. The carbon-oxygen double bond is very strong, and simple aldehydes and ketones absorb at about 1720 cm^{-1} in the infrared, owing to the C=O stretching motion. Conjugation with a double bond or phenyl group reduces the double-bond character of the carbonyl because of resonance, as illustrated above, and such compounds absorb at longer wavelengths, near 1690 cm^{-1}. The olefin stretching frequency is also low for the same reason.

There are also carbonyl compounds analogous to allene, which are highly reactive. They are called ketenes:

$$H_2C\text{=}C\text{=}O$$

ketene

When a molecule contains two or more hydroxyl groups on different carbons, the groups behave more or less independently. Compounds with two hydroxyls on the same carbon are rare. For the most part these decompose spontaneously with the loss of water and yield aldehydes or ketones:

$$
\begin{array}{c}
\text{OH} \\
| \\
\text{R}-\text{C}-\text{OH} \\
| \\
\text{H}
\end{array}
\longrightarrow
\begin{array}{c}
\text{O} \\
\parallel \\
\text{R}-\text{C} \\
\backslash \\
\text{H}
\end{array}
+ \text{H}_2\text{O}
$$

A few stable *n,n*-dihydroxy compounds in which the R is powerfully electron-withdrawing are known; one example is chloral hydrate. Compounds with a hydroxyl and an alkoxyl on the same carbon are called hemiketals (from ketones) or hemiacetals (from aldehydes), and are uncommon in simple systems. Ketals and acetals, which contain two alkoxyls on the same carbon, are stable and well known.

$$
\begin{array}{c}
\text{Cl} \ \ \text{OH} \\
| \ \ \ | \\
\text{Cl}-\text{C}-\text{C}-\text{OH} \\
| \ \ \ | \\
\text{Cl} \ \ \text{H}
\end{array}
\qquad
\begin{array}{c}
\text{OCH}_3 \\
| \\
\text{CH}_3-\text{C}-\text{H} \\
| \\
\text{OCH}_3
\end{array}
\qquad
\begin{array}{c}
\text{OCH}_3 \\
| \\
\text{CH}_3-\text{C}-\text{CH}_3 \\
| \\
\text{OCH}_3
\end{array}
\qquad
\begin{array}{c}
\text{OH} \\
| \\
\text{CH}_3-\text{C}-\text{OCH}_3 \\
| \\
\text{H}
\end{array}
$$

chloral hydrate   an acetal   a ketal   a hemiacetal

The nitrogen analogues of carbonyl compounds are the imines. Aldimines ($\text{R}-\overset{|}{\underset{H}{C}}=\text{NH}$) and ketimines ($\text{R}_2\text{C}=\text{NH}$) are both known. The nitrogen in such compounds is approximately trigonal, and the two trigonal atoms and their substituents, including the nitrogen lone pair, lie in the same plane:

$$
\begin{array}{c}
\text{R} \\
\ \ \ \ \backslash \\
\ \ \ \ \ \ \ \ \text{C}=\text{N} \\
\ \ \ \ / \ \ \ \ \ \ \ \ \backslash \\
\text{R} \ \ \ \ \ \ \ \ \ \ \text{R}
\end{array}
$$

The hydrogen or alkyl on nitrogen can be *cis* or *trans* with respect to the groups on carbon, and isomers of this kind (which are referred to as *syn* and *anti*, for groups on the same and opposite sides, respectively) are known. In a number of other compounds the hydrogen on nitrogen is replaced by various groups. Examples are:

$(\text{CH}_3)_2\text{C}=\text{N}-\text{H}$
acetone imine

$(\text{CH}_3)\text{C}=\text{N}-\text{CH}_3$
N-methyl acetone imine

$(\text{CH}_3)_2\text{C}=\text{NOH}$
acetone oxime

$(\text{CH}_3)_2\text{C}=\text{NNH}_2$
acetone hydrazone

These compounds have miscellaneous uses, but present little that is of structural interest. Triply bonded nitrogens are known in two types of organic molecules, the nitriles and the isonitriles. The latter are among the rare compounds containing divalent carbon:

$$CH_3-C\equiv N$$
acetonitrile

$$CH_3-\overset{\oplus}{N}\equiv\overset{\ominus}{C}: \longleftrightarrow CH_3\ddot{N}=C:$$
an isonitrile

The nitriles are named by the IUPAC system by adding *nitrile* to the end of the name of the appropriate alkane; for example, butanenitrile, $CH_3-CH_2-CH_2-C\equiv N$. The bonding at nitrogen in these compounds is similar to that at carbon in acetylene. The lone pair is in the $2s$ orbital, the p_x orbital forms a σ bond, and the p_y and p_z orbitals form two perpendicular π bonds to the attached carbon.

One or both of the methyls in acetone can be replaced by various other atoms or groups, and this leads to a whole variety of structures. Most such compounds are thought of as derivatives of carboxylic acids, because of the methods by which they are prepared synthetically. The carboxylic acids are as shown. The IUPAC names are not commonly used for the first few members of the series, and they are given in parentheses.

$$\overset{\overset{\displaystyle O}{\|}}{HO-C-OH}$$
carbonic acid

$$\overset{\overset{\displaystyle O}{\|}}{H-C-OH}$$
formic acid
(methanoic acid)

$$\overset{\overset{\displaystyle O}{\|}}{CH_3-C-OH}$$
acetic acid
(ethanoic acid)

$$\overset{\overset{\displaystyle O}{\|}}{CH_3CH_2-C-OH}$$
propionic acid
(propanoic acid)

$$CH_3CH_2CH_2-C\overset{\displaystyle O}{\underset{\displaystyle OH}{\diagup}}$$
butyric acid
(butanoic acid)

⬡—COOH

benzoic acid

⬡—COOH

cyclohexanecarboxylic
acid

The hydroxyl of the acid can be replaced by various electronegative atoms or groups, leading to the acid halides, the acid anhydrides, the esters, and the amides, which have the general formulas RCOX, RCOOCOR', RCOOR' and RCONR'R'', respectively; and are here illustrated by a number of examples:

$$\overset{\overset{\displaystyle O}{\|}}{CH_3-C-Cl}$$
acetyl chloride

benzoic anhydride

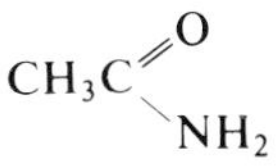

CH$_3$C$\diagdown$^{O} $\diagdown$NH$_2$

acetamide

CH$_3$CH$_2$C$\diagdown$^{O} $\diagdown$O—CH$_3$

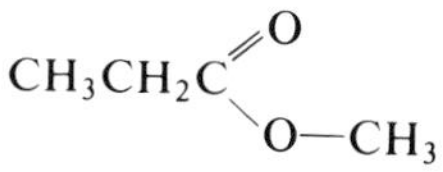

methyl propionate

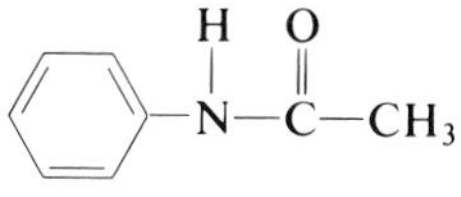

[benzene ring]—N—C—CH$_3$ (with H and O above)

acetanilide

[benzene ring]—C(=O)—O—CHCH$_2$CH$_3$ (with CH$_3$)

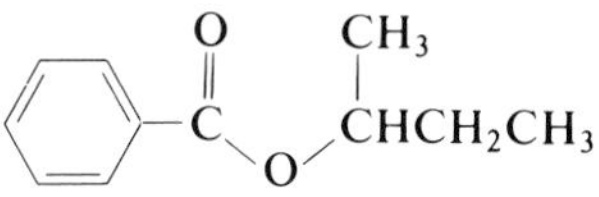

2-butyl benzoate

In each case the attached atom is joined by a σ bond to the carbonyl carbon, by a $2p$ orbital from the halogens, or by a hybrid orbital from nitrogen or oxygen. The situation is a little more complicated than that, however, since there is, to take acetamide as an example, the possibility of putting the lone pair on nitrogen into a p orbital and letting this overlap with the $2p$ orbital on the carbonyl carbon:

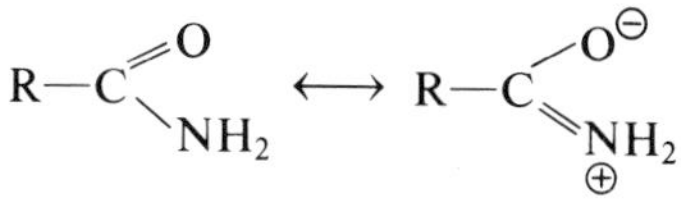

$$R—C\diagdown{}^{O}_{NH_2} \longleftrightarrow R—C\diagdown{}^{O^{\ominus}}_{\overset{+}{N}H_2}$$

Then we have four electrons shared between the three-centered π system, and the carbonyl group, the nitrogen, and all their attached atoms lie in one plane:

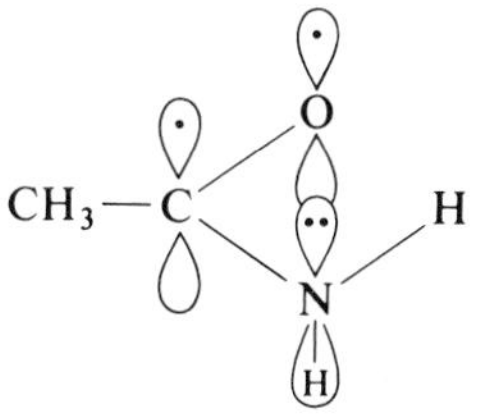

CH$_3$—C (orbital diagram with O, N, H)

Recall that ammonia is pyramidal rather than planar, although the energy difference between the forms is not very large. Here the extra conjugation energy is sufficient to make the planar (sp^2) form of the nitrogen the more stable. Nitrogen, being less electronegative than oxygen, undergoes this kind of resonance the better of the two; fluorine is poorer than either. In terms of resonance forms, the ionic form is of decreasing importance relative to the covalent form in the series:

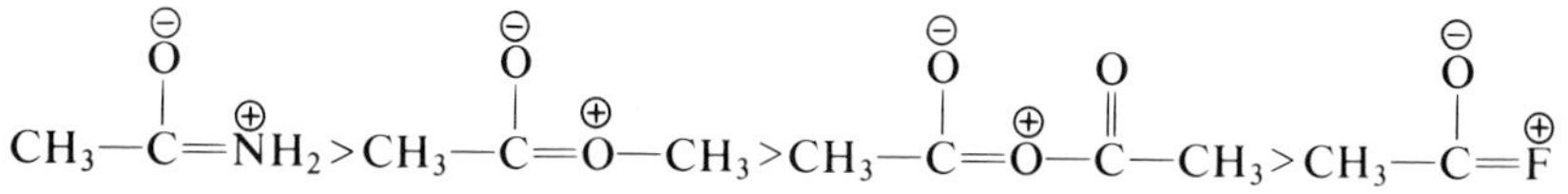

$$CH_3—\overset{\overset{\ominus}{O}}{C}=\overset{+}{N}H_2 > CH_3—\overset{\overset{\ominus}{O}}{C}=\overset{+}{O}—CH_3 > CH_3—\overset{\overset{\ominus}{O}}{C}=\overset{+}{O}—\overset{O}{C}—CH_3 > CH_3—\overset{\overset{\ominus}{O}}{C}=\overset{+}{F}$$

The amount of single-bond character in the carbonyl group decreases along the series, and the amount of double-bond character increases. The carbonyl stretching frequencies consequently increase from about 1690 cm^{-1} for amides to 1740 cm^{-1} for esters to 1800 cm^{-1} for acid halides and anhydrides (the latter is actually a doublet from the coupling of the two carbonyl vibrations).

The carboxylic acids are stronger than the weakly acidic phenols and mercaptans, but still not as strong as the mineral acids. The main reason for their appreciable acidity is the stability of the anion. The carboxylate anion has two equivalent resonance forms:

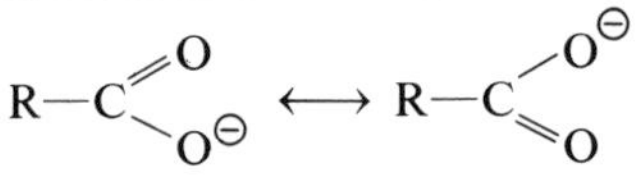

A whole variety of nitrogen compounds is known in which a nitrogen atom is singly or multiply bonded to another nitrogen, or to an oxygen, or to both:

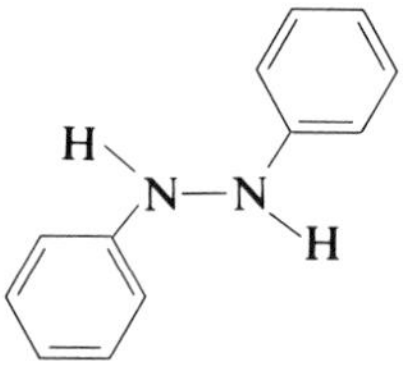

hydrazobenzene

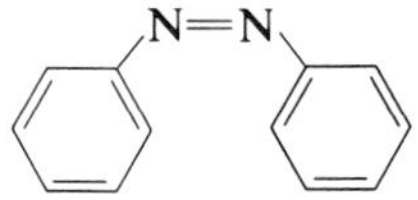

cis-azobenzene

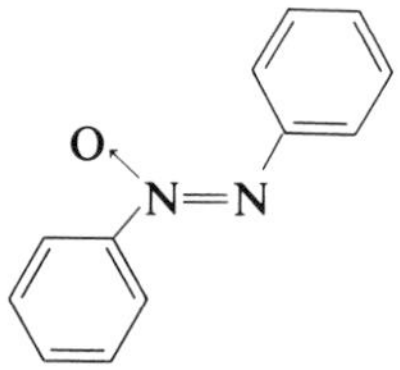

trans-azoxybenzene

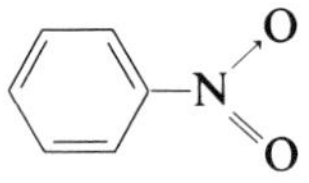

nitrobenzene

The structures are for the most part predictable by analogy to the corresponding carbon analogues. Unusual features are to be found in azoxybenzene and nitrobenzene. The former is obtained by allowing azobenzene (a Lewis base) to donate the lone pair from one nitrogen to an oxygen atom (a Lewis acid). The resulting nitrogen-oxygen linkage is referred to as a *semipolar double bond* or a *coordinate covalence*, and is often represented by an arrow in the direction of the electron donation (see the structures above). In nitrobenzene the same kind of bonding exists, but here the oxygens are equivalent because of resonance. In all these groups there are various kinds of possibilities for resonance with the conjugated systems. If the nitrogen orbital conjugated to phenyl is an unfilled π orbital, electrons will be withdrawn from phenyl, as shown for nitrobenzene:

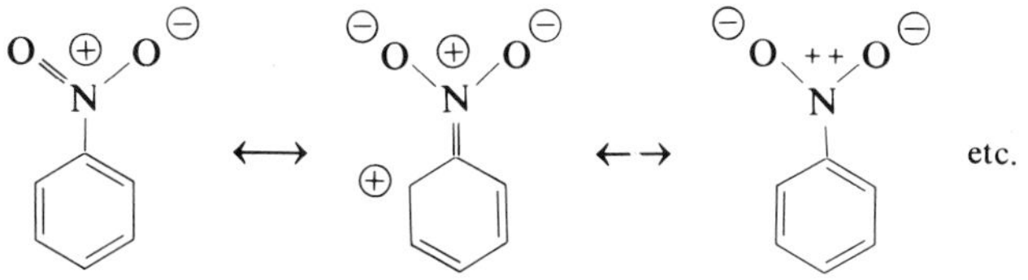

If the lone pair in its isolated orbital is conjugated with phenyl, as in aniline, hydrazobenzene, and phenylhydroxylamine, the phenyl withdraws electrons:

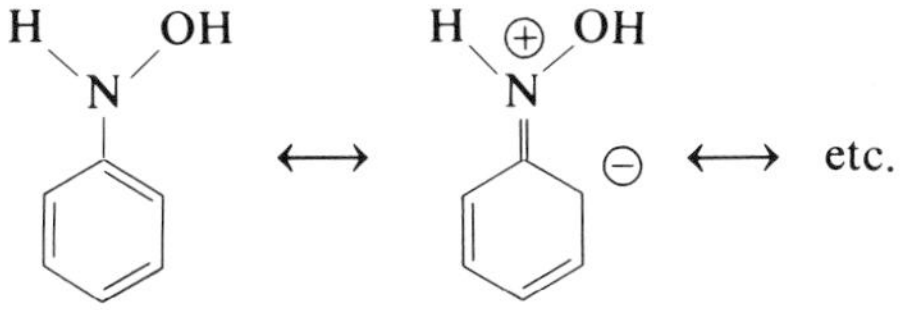

There are a number of types of organic sulfur compounds in which the sulfur has a valence of greater than 2; some examples are the following (the phenyl group is often represented by the symbol ϕ):

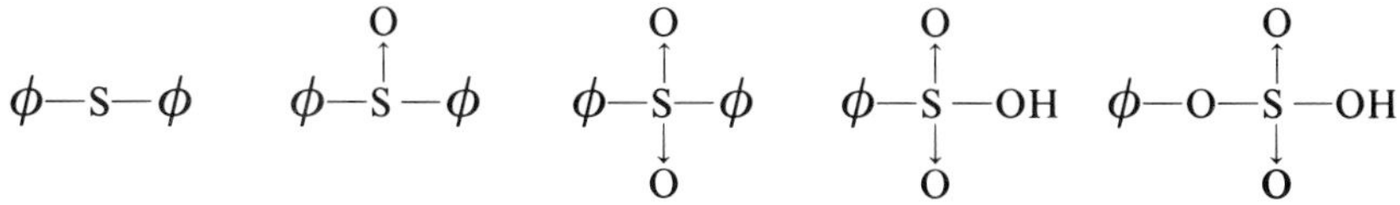

| diphenyl sulfide | diphenyl sulfoxide | diphenyl sulfone | benzenesulfonic acid | phenyl hydrogen sulfate |

The sulfur atom in diphenyl sulfide can form a coordinate covalent bond to an oxygen atom, which gives a sulfoxide. The sulfur atom in a sulfoxide is pyramidal, but it does not invert spontaneously, as does the nitrogen in ammonia. Consequently, if there are two different groups attached to the sulfur in a sulfoxide, the oxygen and lone pair allow the the existence of enantiomers, and such compounds are known in optically active form. The next higher oxidation product is the sulfone; in this compound there is a formal double positive charge on sulfur and, while such a situation is very unfavorable with the small atoms in the first row of the periodic table, it is satisfactory here. The next higher oxidation state is that of a sulfonic acid; these acids are strong acids, similar to sulfuric. Monoesters and diesters of sulfuric acid (sulfate esters) are also known, as are acids of sulfur where the latter has lower oxidation states.

5.5 HETEROCYCLIC COMPOUNDS

If all the ring atoms in a cyclic compound are the same (usually carbon), the compound is referred to as alicyclic or homocyclic. If there are two or more kinds of atoms in the ring, the compound is said to be

heterocyclic. A trivial system of nomenclature is widely used for heterocyclic systems, and it is based on rings which are as unsaturated as possible. The more common aromatic heterocycles are:

pyridine   pyrazine   pyran   pyrrole

furan   thiophene   thiazole

Pyridine is structurally similar to benzene, in that the nitrogen furnishes
a p orbital and one electron to the π system. Instead of having an attached
hydrogen, the lone pair is in an orbital hybridized approximately sp^2.
There are two Kekulé forms of pyridine, and the compound is similar to
benzene in many respects. Pyran is not aromatic, as the conjugation is
interrupted, but is just an unsaturated ether.

pyridine   pyrrole

Pyrrole has a somewhat more unusual structure. Here the nitrogen does
have a hydrogen or substituent attached to it, and also it furnishes an
electron pair to the π system. The π systems in both pyridine and pyrrole
contain six electrons. Thus, these systems follow Hückel's rule (Sec. 4.4),
and they are stable (aromatic) systems. Only one Kekulé form can be
written for pyrrole, but there are four charged forms, all of which together
yield a resonance-stabilized system:

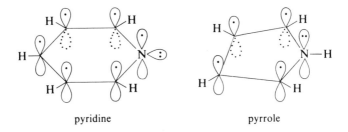

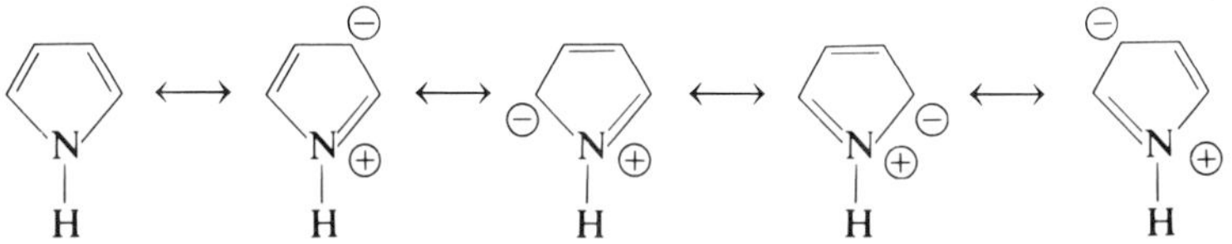

Note that in pyrrole resonance tends to put the electrons on nitrogen and take them out of the ring and away from the carbon atoms, whereas in pyrrole it puts electrons into the ring. The result is that, whereas the pyridine ring is quite reactive toward Lewis bases, it is quite unreactive with Lewis acids, and pyrrole tends to be reactive toward Lewis acids and unreactive with Lewis bases. Furan and thiophene are roughly similar to pyrrole in many respects.

There are a large number of five- and six-membered ring systems containing one, two, or even more heteroatoms in all kinds of combinations, but they present no special structural features. Hydrogenated derivatives of the various aromatic heterocycles are similar to their acyclic counterparts:

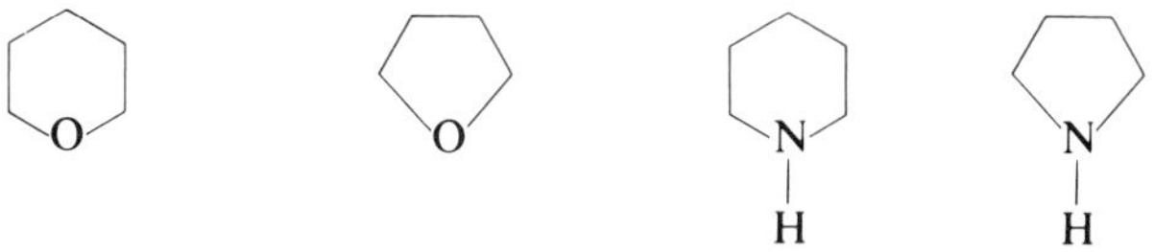

| tetrahydropyran | tetrahydrofuran | piperidine | pyrrolidine |

5.6 NUCLEAR MAGNETIC RESONANCE AND INFRARED SPECTRA

In Chaps. 3 and 4 the basis for the determination of structure by the NMR method and some of the applications to hydrocarbons were outlined. The chemical shifts found for a proton vary with its environment, and now that this variation is pretty well understood, from a study of many compounds of known structure, we can use the NMR spectrum of any compound to help establish its structure. In general, the more electrons are withdrawn from around a proton, the lower the field (τ value) at which it will be observed. A summary of the τ values typical for several common structural types is given in Table 5-1. Very extensive tabulations of this sort have been made.

Table 5-1

TYPICAL τ VALUES FOR PROTONS OF VARIOUS TYPES

Type	τ	Type	τ
$-SO_3H$	$-1.7^{\dagger}$	$-ROH$	$+5.1^{\dagger}$
$-COOH$	$-1.4^{\dagger}$	$-OCH_3$	$+6.8$
$R-CHO$	$+0.5$	$\equiv C-H$	$+7.6$
$RCONH_2$	$+2.3$	$\equiv C-CH_3$	$+8.5$
$ArOH$	$+2.9^{\dagger}$	$-CH_2-$	$+8.7$
ArH	$+2.7$	$R-NH_2$	$+8.8^{\dagger}$
$=CH_2$	$+4.6$	$C-CH_3$	$+9.1$

$^{\dagger}\tau$ values quite variable.

The acids might be expected to have a minimum of electron density around their acidic protons, and this is what is found. Sulfonic acids show resonance near $-1.7\ \tau$; the resonance of the carboxylic acids is not quite so far down, near $-1.4\ \tau$. The less acidic compounds (phenols, alcohols, and hydrocarbons) are observed progressively upfield, as anticipated. The olefinic protons come rather far downfield compared with the aliphatic ones, as mentioned earlier, and the aldehyde proton is even farther down because of the strong electron withdrawing effect of the oxygen, both by resonance and by induction. One might think from the τ value that such an aldehydic hydrogen would be acidic; it is not, however, because a hydrogen is acidic only if the anion formed by its removal is reasonably stable. The anion which would result from removal of the aldehydic hydrogen would not be very stable because the charge would be on a carbon atom, and it could not resonate.

The methyl group attached to carbon is seen near $9.1\ \tau$. If it is attached to more electronegative atoms (as in propene or methanol), it is seen at lower field.

The reason for the shift of an aromatic proton downfield relative to an olefinic one was mentioned in Sec. 4.4. The acetylenic proton is shifted upfield for a similar reason. In an acetylene the current is through the π system, around a ring perpendicular to the C—C σ bond. The proton on benzene is outside the ring current, in acetylene it is inside, and the resulting shifts are in the opposite directions.

A summary of some of the more useful infrared absorption frequencies is given in Table 5-2.

In the practical problem of determining the structure of a molecule, there are usually three pieces of information which are desired at the outset. These are the molecular formula and the infrared and NMR spectra. The formula tells what atoms are present, the infrared spectrum tells how these atoms are combined into the functional groups present and, if the molecule is not too complicated, the NMR spectrum shows the molecular skeleton and the locations of these func-

Table 5-2

INFRARED SPECTRAL CORRELATIONS

Structure	Approximate absorption frequencies (cm^{-1})[†]
—CH_2—	2850 (s), 2900 (s)
—CH_3	2850 (s), 2950 (s), 1390 (s)
C=C—H	3100 (m)
C≡C—H	3300 (m)
CHO	2800 (s)
COOH	3600 (m), 2500–2800 (bonded)
—OH	3600 (free), 2500–3500 (bonded)
—NH_2	3400 (m)
—C≡N	2250 (s)
C=C=C	1980 (m)
C=C	1650 (w)
C=N	1680 (w)
C—NO_2	1530 (s), 1350 (s)
Satd. ketones and acids	1720(s)
α, β unsatd. ketones	1680(s)
Satd. aldehydes	1730(s)
Acid halides	1790(s)
Amides	1620–1700(s)
C—OH	1020–1180(s), 1250–1410(s)

[†]A rough guide to intensity is given: (s) = strong; (m) = medium, (w) = weak.

tional groups. In the case of large molecules, having, say, twenty carbons or more, the NMR spectrum usually presents such a jumble of unresolved bands that the exact structure cannot be assigned with certainty, but often it can be limited to a certain small number of possibilities and then many other techniques can be applied to determine the exact structure (for example, the x-ray method). It may turn out that the compound is closely related to a compound of known structure; in such a case, usually the easiest approach is to convert one to the other and thereby determine the structure of the unknown one.

Often the easiest approach to the determination of the structure of a large molecule is chemically to break the molecule into two or more smaller molecules, and these may be relatively easy to identify. The methods used in breaking apart the large molecule will probably suggest how the pieces should fit together. At the present time a method for bringing about this breakage by means of electron bombardment is being developed; under the proper conditions the molecule can be broken into a great many fragments. A molecule of the type A—B—C—D may break down to give A, B, C, D, A—B, B—C, C—D, A—B—C, etc. The fragments are sorted out by means of an instrument called a mass spectrometer, which determines the masses, or molecular weights, of the fragments and their relative amounts. The fragments are then put together mentally like a jig-saw puzzle and, hopefully, the structure is determined.

5.7 POLYFUNCTIONAL COMPOUNDS

Many molecules of interest contain two or more functional groups. There are two sets of rules for the nomenclature of aromatic compounds, which we may note at this point. The systematic nomenclature has a numbering system around the aromatic ring, the numbering beginning with 1 at the carbon containing the substituent which leads to the basic name of the compound, but this number is understood and not included in the name:

2-fluorophenol

4-bromobenzoic acid

2-hydroxy-4-bromobenzoic acid

Thus, for 2-fluorophenol, it is understood that the hydroxyl (phenol) is at 1. The numbering proceeds in the direction which yields the lowest num-

ber (2-fluorophenol, not 6-fluorophenol). If there are exactly two substituents on a benzene ring, the compounds are often called *ortho, meta,*
or *para,* depending on whether the substituents are 1,2 or 1,3, or 1,4,
respectively:

o-nitrophenol   *m*-dibromobenzene

In general, if two substituents are not conjugated with one another
they behave more or less independently (if close together they are not
completely independent because of induction, as discussed below). If two
substituents are conjugated with one another, either by direct attachment
or by proper (vinylogous) attachment to an unsaturated system, conspicuous alterations in their properties occur. The *o-, m-,* and *p*-cyano-
anilines will serve as illustrations of resonance possibilities between two
substituents. There are various resonance forms for aniline (Sec. 5.3) and
for benzonitrile. The *m*-cyanoaniline shows only the same kinds of forms,
there is no conjugation between the substituents, and this is always true
of *m*-isomers:

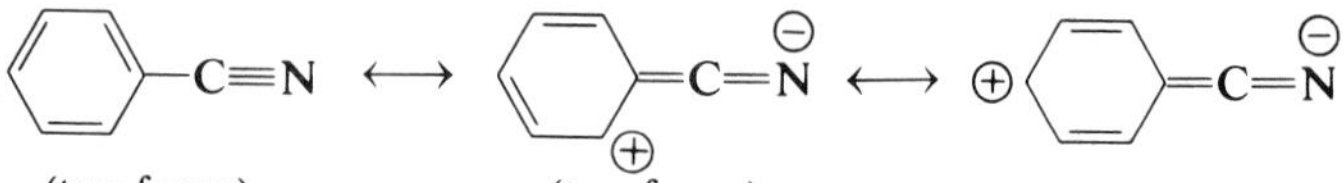

(two forms)   (two forms)

The *ortho* and *para* isomers all have the same kinds of resonance forms
as do the *meta* and, in addition, they have forms which involve both substituents simultaneously:

This extra resonance is significant in compounds in which there is one
electron-donating group and one electron-withdrawing group, either *ortho*
or *para* to one another, as in *p*-nitrophenol, *o*-fluorobenzonitrile, *p*-
methoxybenzoic acid, etc.

Dipole moments provide a convenient method of detecting this resonance. Recall that a molecule like H—F possesses a dipole moment
because the centers of positive and negative charge do not coincide.
Dipole moments are vectors and have both magnitude (measured in debye
units, D) and direction, and they are often represented by arrows pointing
toward the negative end of the dipole: H $\longrightarrow$ F. If any two groups are
meta to one another on the benzene ring, their resultant dipole moment
is close to that calculated by vector addition of the group moments, so
the interaction between the groups is small. The same is found to be true

when the groups are *para*, if both groups are electron-attracting or if both are electron-donating. Thus, *m*- and *p*-dibromobenzene have dipole moments close to what one would calculate by vector addition:

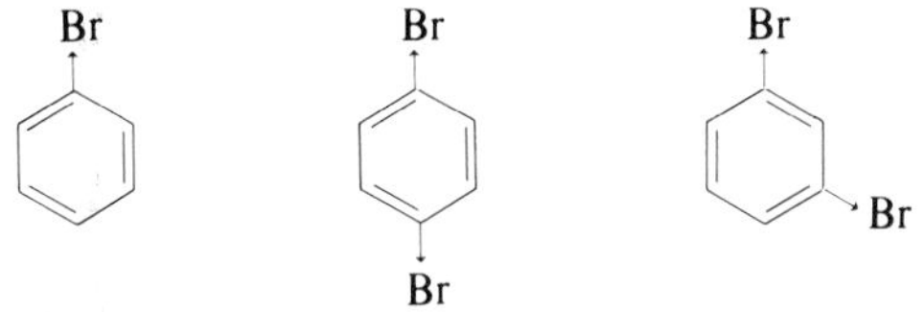

1.5 D   0 D   1.5 D

If an electron-donating group is located *para* to an electron-attracting group, this simple additivity of the vectors does not hold. The observed dipole moment is, in fact, considerably greater than that calculated by adding the group vectors. This observed increase results because the new highly polar resonance form contributes to the hybrid. For example, the moment of *p*-aminonitrobenzene can be calculated by vector addition, as indicated below,

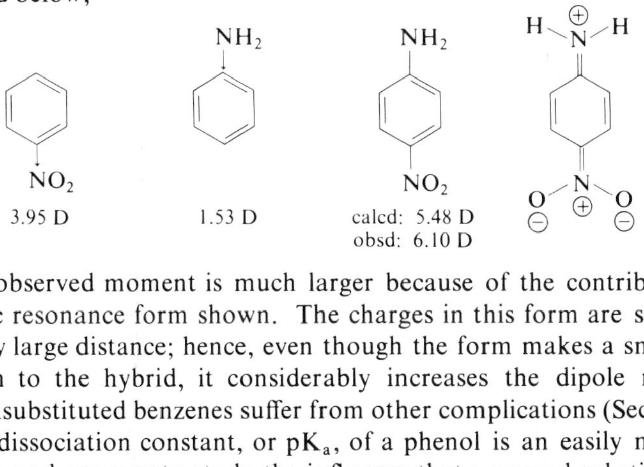

3.95 D   1.53 D   calcd: 5.48 D
                             obsd: 6.10 D

but the observed moment is much larger because of the contribution of the ionic resonance form shown. The charges in this form are separated by a very large distance; hence, even though the form makes a small contribution to the hybrid, it considerably increases the dipole moment. *Ortho*-disubstituted benzenes suffer from other complications (Sec. 6.5).

The dissociation constant, or pK_a, of a phenol is an easily measured quantity, and one way to study the influence that a second substituent on the benzene ring has on the hydroxyl is to measure the pK_a of the substituted phenol. The substituent may exert a resonance effect; consider *p*-nitrosophenol, for example:

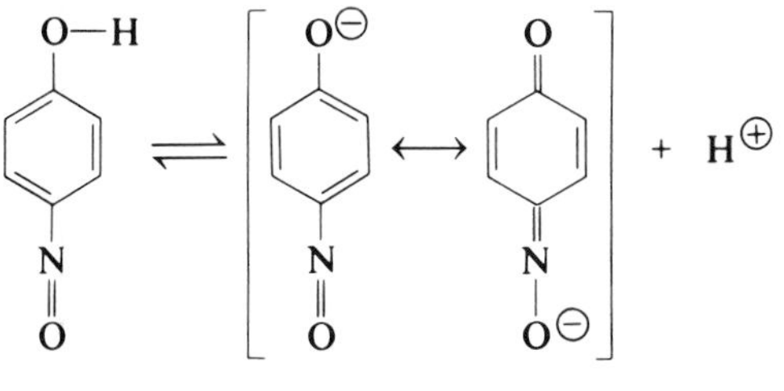

Resonance stabilizes the phenolate anion very much more than the phenol itself, especially because of the resonance shown. It is found that *p*-

nitrosophenol is, in fact, a very much stronger acid than phenol itself, as predicted.

What can we predict about the acidity of *m*-fluorophenol? Since the groups are *meta*, there is no direct resonance interaction. If *m*-fluoro-phenol differs in acidity from phenol, the difference must be attributed to an inductive effect, and we can now examine the nature of this effect in detail. Since the force exerted by a charge decreases with distance, the inductive effect of a dipole varies with the distances of the positive and negative centers from the reaction site. The difference in the acidity of phenol and *m*-fluorophenol depends primarily on whether the fluorine makes the charge on the oxygen in the anion more or less stable, as dis-cussed in Sec. 4.2. The fluorine atom is the negative end of the dipole. The carbon to which the fluorine is attached is the positive end and, since it is closer to the oxygen than is the fluorine, it will exert a larger effect. The positive carbon makes the anion more stable, and hence *m*-fluoro-phenol is more acidic than phenol itself.

Will *p*-fluorophenol be more or less acidic than phenol or than the *meta* isomer? This question is more difficult to answer, because with the *para* isomer both inductive and resonance effects must be considered. The distance and orientation of the C—F dipole with respect to oxygen are roughly similar in the *meta* and *para* isomers, so the inductive effect of the C—F dipole is also similar.

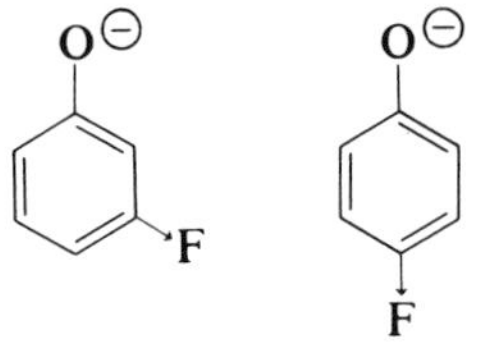

The fluorine can put electrons into the aromatic ring by resonance, which lowers the energy of the molecule.

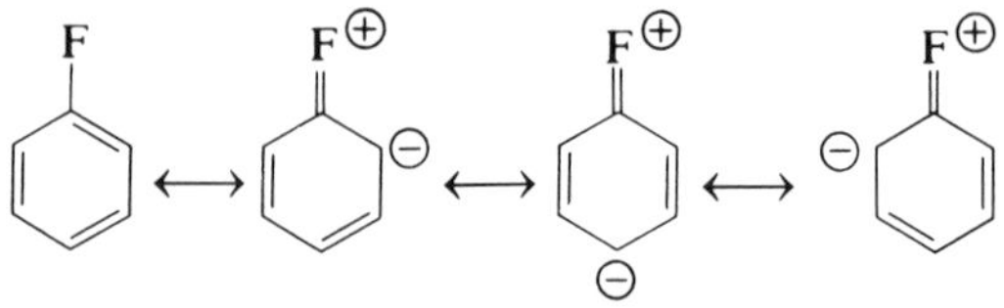

One of these resonance forms in the *p*-fluorophenol anion has two nega-tive charges on adjacent atoms and is consequently unfavorable:

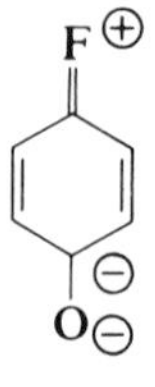

Resonance occurs only when it will stabilize a system. If, as in this case, such a form does not stabilize the system, resonance will not occur. This resonance will occur in the undissociated phenol but not in the anion and will, therefore, shift the equilibrium toward the phenol. Hence the resonance effect will make *p*-fluorophenol a weaker acid than it would be if there were no resonance. The inductive effect is tending to make it stronger, and the balance relative to the unsubstituted phenol cannot be predicted without numerical data. The *p*-fluorophenol will, however, be a weaker acid than the *meta* isomer.

We may note that most groups are electron-withdrawing, both by induction and by resonance:

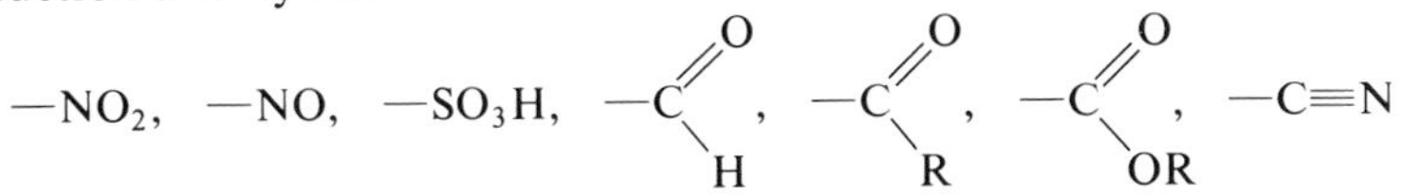

$$-NO_2, \quad -NO, \quad -SO_3H, \quad -C\overset{\displaystyle O}{\underset{\displaystyle H}{\big\backslash}}, \quad -C\overset{\displaystyle O}{\underset{\displaystyle R}{\big\backslash}}, \quad -C\overset{\displaystyle O}{\underset{\displaystyle OR}{\big\backslash}}, \quad -C\equiv N$$

The amino group is the most important electron-donating group. The halogens and oxygen (phenol) withdraw electrons by induction, but donate them by resonance. The halogens are therefore powerful electron-withdrawing groups if in the *meta* position but weak withdrawing groups in the *para* position, because of the partial compensation of the withdrawing effect by the resonance effect. The oxygen atom in phenol is actually an electron-withdrawing group when *meta* but a donor when *para*. Thus, *m*-methoxybenzoic acid is a stronger acid than benzoic, but the *para* isomer is weaker. In the latter compound, resonance stabilizes the acid more than the anion, and the acid is therefore weaker than benzoic acid:

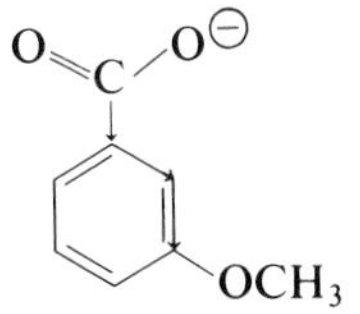

more stable ion,   less stable ion,
stronger acid   weaker acid

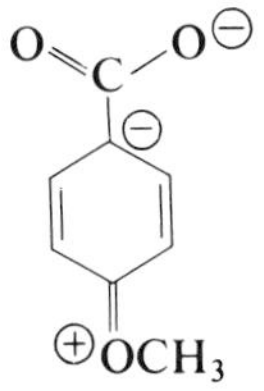

5.8 FATS, CARBOHYDRATES, AND PROTEINS

A number of compounds that are of biological importance are commonly referred to as fats. These compounds are esters of glycerol and straight-chain aliphatic carboxylic acids, usually long-chain acids with an even number of carbon atoms such as palmitic or stearic or, in the case of unsaturated fats, oleic:

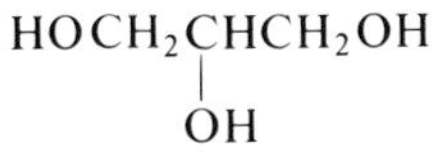

$$HOCH_2CHCH_2OH \qquad\qquad CH_3(CH_2)_{14}COOH$$
$$\underset{\displaystyle OH}{|}$$

glycerol   palmitic acid

$$CH_3(CH_2)_7CH=CH(CH_2)_7COOH \qquad\qquad CH_3(CH_2)_{16}COOH$$
oleic acid (cis isomer)   stearic acid

Depending on the source of the fat, R, R′, and R″ may all be the same or different (usually combinations of the acids shown, plus smaller amounts of a few others):

$$CH_2\!\!-\!\!O\!\!-\!\!\overset{\displaystyle O}{\overset{\displaystyle \|}{C}}\!\!-\!\!R$$

$$CH\ \ \!\!-\!\!O\!\!-\!\!\overset{\displaystyle O}{\overset{\displaystyle \|}{C}}\!\!-\!\!R'$$

$$CH_2\!\!-\!\!O\!\!-\!\!\overset{\displaystyle O}{\overset{\displaystyle \|}{C}}\!\!-\!\!R''$$

a fat

From the point of view of structure, the fats are not significantly different from other esters.

The carbohydrates, compounds of the formula $(CH_2O)_n$, make up a class of naturally occurring compounds of considerable importance. The common monosaccharides (sugars) are called hexoses or pentoses, indicating that they contain six or five carbons respectively. They contain one carbonyl group, usually an aldehyde, and a hydroxyl group on each of the remaining carbons. Glucose is a typical example, and it is the sugar found most commonly in nature.

CHO	CH₂OH	CHO	CHO
H—C—OH	C=O	HO—C—H	HO—C—H
HO—C—H	HO—C—H	HO—C—H	H—C—OH
H—C—OH	H—C—OH	H—C—OH	HO—C—H
H—C—OH	H—C—OH	H—C—OH	HO—C—H
CH₂OH	CH₂OH	CH₂OH	CH₂OH
D-glucose	D-fructose	D-mannose	L-glucose

Inspection of the formula of glucose shows that it contains four asymmetric carbons and hence is one of sixteen possible stereoisomers. The problem of isomers in the sugars is quite formidable. For a biochemical process in which D-glucose is required, none of its isomers will suffice.

Trivial names are used almost exclusively for the sugars; thus, D- and L-glucose are enantiomers and the other diastereomers have different names. The D forms are most common in nature, and the D or L designation is arrived at by comparing the configuration of the asymmetric carbon farthest from the carbonyl group with D- or L-glyceraldehyde, whose configurations are known.

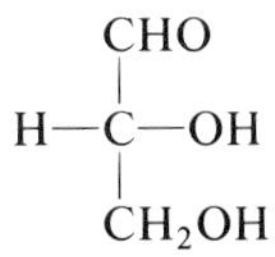

$$\begin{array}{c} CHO \\ | \\ H-C-OH \\ | \\ CH_2OH \end{array} \qquad\qquad \begin{array}{c} CHO \\ | \\ HO-C-H \\ | \\ CH_2OH \end{array}$$

D-glyceraldehyde 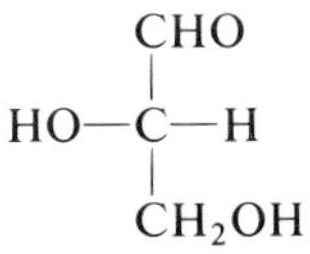   L-glyceraldehyde

The sugars can be used to illustrate the influence of two functional groups on each other, as well as a general fact of organic chemistry, namely that the formation of five- or six-membered rings tends to be a relatively favorable process. The result is that equilibria involving such a ring on one side of the equation tend to be shifted in that direction, relative to their acyclic counterparts, and reactions that proceed through such cyclic intermediates proceed more rapidly than similar reactions which do not. This difference between cyclic and acyclic systems is a result of a quantity called the entropy of the system. Entropy is simply a measure of disorder or confusion. Nature tends to become more and more disordered, and entropy tends to increase. Thus, processes which lead to more disorder are favored over similar ones which do not.

Recall the earlier discussion of hemiacetal formation, in which it was stated that it is difficult to prepare simple acyclic hemiacetals. The equilibrium for the following reaction

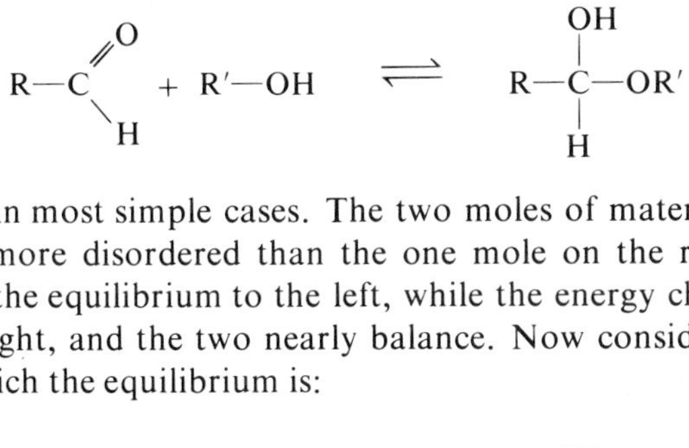

$$R-C\!\!\begin{array}{c} {}^{O} \\ {}_{H} \end{array} + R'-OH \;\rightleftharpoons\; \begin{array}{c} OH \\ | \\ R-C-OR' \\ | \\ H \end{array}$$

lies to the left in most simple cases. The two moles of material on the left can be much more disordered than the one mole on the right. Entropy tends to push the equilibrium to the left, while the energy change is pushing it to the right, and the two nearly balance. Now consider the case of glucose, in which the equilibrium is:

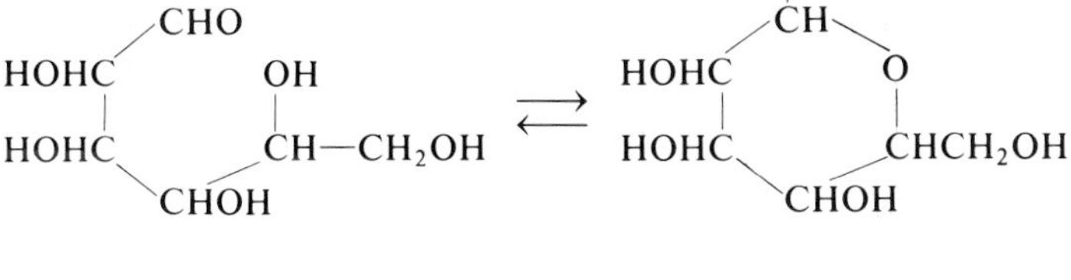

$$\begin{array}{c} \quad\;\; CHO \\ HOHC \qquad OH \\ | \qquad\qquad | \\ HOHC \qquad CH-CH_2OH \\ \quad\; CHOH \end{array} \;\rightleftharpoons\; \begin{array}{c} \quad\;\;\; OH \\ \quad\;\; CH \\ HOHC \qquad O \\ | \qquad\qquad | \\ HOHC \qquad CHCH_2OH \\ \quad\; CHOH \end{array}$$

The energy change here is similar to the acyclic case, and pushes the equilibrium to the right. The entropy loss which is so unfavorable in the acyclic case, that of going from two molecules to one, does not affect the situation here. Hence glucose and most simple sugars are found to exist as hemiacetals, and they do not show carbonyl stretching absorption in their infrared spectra. In general, five- and six-membered rings form easily because they do not involve the great entropy loss associated with the combining of two molecules, as in acyclic systems. Smaller rings are very strained and do not tend to form easily (Sec. 4.4), and large rings suffer another type of strain (Sec. 6.3) which makes them relatively unstable. The five- and six-membered rings are therefore special cases, in which the energy of their formation is not unfavorable compared with their acyclic analogues, and the entropy of their formation is much more favorable.than in the corresponding acyclic change. Hence, as a general rule, five- and six-membered rings tend to form if they can.

Since the sugars exist as hemiacetals, it is more accurate to picture them as such (by convention, the heavy portion of the ring is nearer the viewer):

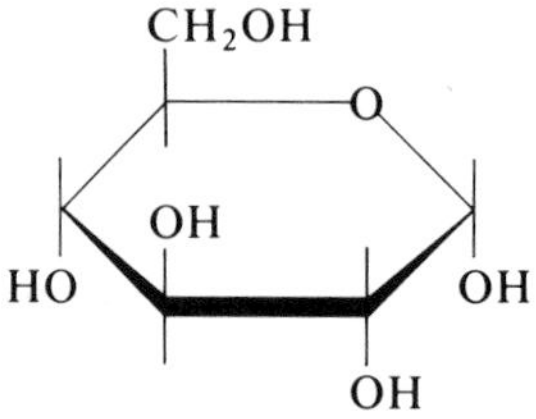

α-D-glucose β-D-mannose

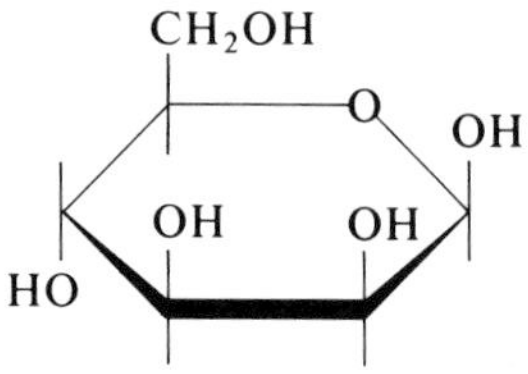

Two of the most common substances in the plant kingdom are cellulose and starch. They are both polymers of glucose, and are referred to as polysaccharides. Upon hydrolysis, both cellulose and starch furnish only D-glucose.

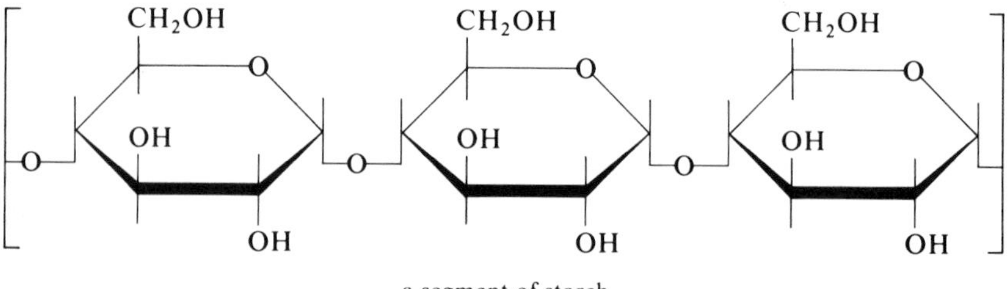

a segment of starch

In both cellulose and starch the molecules are quite large, their molecular weights being, though variable, in the range of 10^5 to 10^6. One major difference between them is that starch has the D-glucose units joined 1,4 by α-glycosidic linkages, while in cellulose the linkages are β. Biologically there is a considerable difference, of course, since we can eat and digest starch (potatoes, corn, and the like) but not cellulose (grass, wood, and cotton).

Exceedingly important groups of naturally occurring compounds are the α-amino acids[†], and their polymers, the polypeptides and proteins. There are twenty common amino acids found as constituents of proteins, all of which have the L-configuration. There are found elsewhere in nature, mainly in plants and in microorganisms, a number of less common amino acids, some of which have the D-configuration. A few of the more common amino acids are shown as they are usually written:

$$\begin{array}{c} \text{COOH} \\ | \\ \text{H}_2\text{N}-\text{C}-\text{H} \\ | \\ \text{H} \end{array}$$
glycine

$$\begin{array}{c} \text{COOH} \\ | \\ \text{H}_2\text{N}-\text{C}-\text{H} \\ | \\ \text{CH}_3 \end{array}$$
alanine

$$\begin{array}{c} \text{COOH} \\ | \\ \text{H}_2\text{N}-\text{C}-\text{H} \\ | \\ \text{CH}_2 \\ | \\ \text{CH}_2 \\ | \\ \text{COOH} \end{array}$$
glutamic acid

$$\begin{array}{c} \text{COOH} \\ | \\ \text{H}_2\text{N}-\text{C}-\text{H} \\ | \\ \text{CH}_2\text{OH} \end{array}$$
serine

$$\begin{array}{c} \text{COOH} \\ | \\ \text{H}_2\text{N}-\text{C}-\text{H} \\ | \\ \text{CH}_2\text{SH} \end{array}$$
cysteine

Under ordinary circumstances they in fact exist as internal salts called zwitterions, or dipolar ions:

$$\overset{\oplus}{\text{H}_3\text{N}}-\text{CH}_2-\text{COO}^{\ominus}$$

This is further illustration of the effect of two functional groups on each other, in this case an amino and a carboxyl group. These compounds in general show the properties of ions, in that they are nonvolatile and water-soluble.

Two or more amino acids can combine via an amide linkage, and the resulting compound is referred to as a dipeptide, tripeptide, etc. depending on the number of amino acid residues involved:

$$\begin{array}{c} \quad\quad\quad\quad \text{O} \\ \quad\quad\quad\quad || \\ \text{H}_2\text{NCH}_2\text{C}-\text{NH}-\text{CH}_2\text{COOH} \end{array}$$
glycylglycine, a dipeptide

$$\begin{array}{c} \quad\quad\quad \text{O} \quad\quad\quad\quad \text{O} \quad\quad\quad\quad \text{O} \\ \quad\quad\quad || \quad\quad\quad\quad || \quad\quad\quad\quad || \\ \text{H}_2\text{NCH}_2\text{C}-\text{NH}-\text{CH}-\text{C}-\text{NH}-\text{CH}-\text{C}-\text{OH} \\ \quad\quad\quad\quad\quad\quad | \quad\quad\quad\quad\quad\quad | \\ \quad\quad\quad\quad\quad\quad \text{CH}_3 \quad\quad\quad\quad \text{CH}_2\text{OH} \end{array}$$
glycylalanylserine, a tripeptide

Large naturally occurring polypeptides with molecular weights of more than 10,000 are referred to as proteins. They are constituents of all

---

[†] The carbon attached to the carboxyl is often referred to as the α-carbon.

living cells, and make up a large part of an animal body, being the principal constituents of blood, skin, nerves, and muscles. Enzymes, the essential organic catalysts which allow life processes to proceed at sufficient rates, are proteins. In most cases proteins consist of one or a few polypeptide chains associated with small amounts (ocasionally with large amounts) of other types of structure. Hemoglobin from blood is an example of a protein that contains a heme group (an iron atom and a large heterocyclic ring system), in addition to the polypeptide chains. Other proteins exist which are combined with carbohydrates (glycoproteins), lipids (lipoproteins), and so on.

The number of different proteins that can be constructed from the twenty most common amino acids is extremely large: since the first amino acid in the chain can be any of 20, as can the second, the number of dipeptides possible is 20^2. Similarly, the number of possible tripeptides is 20^3. For a protein containing 200 amino acid units, there are 20^{200} different possibilities! It is thought that there are about one hundred thousand specific kinds of proteins required to operate a typical animal body, and most of these differ for different species of animals. The complexity of a living creature is staggering from this aspect alone.

Determination of the *primary* structure (the amino-acid sequence) of a large peptide or protein is a formidable task. One of the most complicated of these molecules that has been tackled successfully is ribonuclease; it consists of a single chain containing 124 amino acid residues, the exact sequence of which is now known.

The primary structure of proteins appears to be solved in principle, but actually to determine the sequence in just one protein requires many man-years of work, and it is clear that real progress will require much more rapid methods than those now available.

The three-dimensional structure of a protein is not determined just by knowing the order in which the amino acids are joined together, because the resulting chain could be coiling and twisting in all sorts of different ways; this subject will be taken up in Chap. 6.

5.9 PROBLEMS

1. (a) Define Lewis acid and Lewis base. (b) What are the formal charges on the elements in bold-face type in the following compounds?

$$(CH_3)_3 \mathbf{N} \rightarrow O \qquad CH_3 {-} \mathbf{N} {=} N \qquad CH_3 {-} \overset{\displaystyle O}{\underset{\displaystyle O}{\mathbf{S}}} {-} OH$$

2. (a) What are the rules for predicting hybridization? Show how they apply to $(CH_3)_3 B$ and $(CH_3)_3 N$. (b) Orbitals from carbon form bonds of varying strengths, depending largely on hybridization. List in order the bond strengths of bonds formed from s, p, and sp^3 orbitals. Explain.

3. (a) Draw the π and σ orbitals (1) of pyridine and (2) of thiazole. (b) Draw the resonance forms of the same compounds.

4. A compound has the formula C_5H_8O. The infrared spectrum shows strong bands at 2900, 1680, and 960 cm^{-1}, and weaker bands at 1390 and 1670 cm^{-1}. The NMR spectrum is as shown. What is the structure?

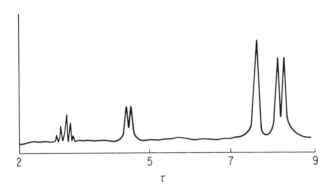

5. From the dipole moment data on page 83 and the law of cosines, calculate the moment of *m*-nitroaniline.

6. Will *p*-carboethoxylaniline be a stronger or weaker base than aniline? Explain.

7. Why is the hydrate formed by the addition of water to Cl_3CCHO so much more stable than the one from H_3CCHO?

8. A compound $C_7H_{12}O$ has absorption in the infrared spectrum at 1390 (s), 3100 (m), 1650 (s), 1150 (s) cm^{-1}, and no absorption between 1660 and 1730 cm^{-1}. The high-resolution NMR spectrum is as shown. What is its structure?

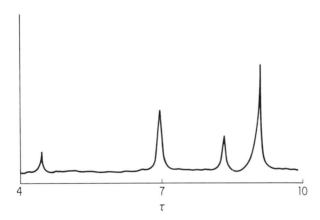

9. (a) Why does glucose form a hemiacetal so readily? (b) Write the Fischer projection formulas for the aldehyde forms of the eight aldopentoses, and indicate which are enantiomers and which are diastereomers.

SUGGESTED READINGS

Additional information on the structures of organic molecules (and simple in-organic ones) presented from the theoretical viewpoint may be found in C. A. Coulson, *Valence*, 2nd ed., London, Clarendon, 1961. Chemical aspects of the subject are covered in O. L. Chapman, *Functional Groups in Organic Chemistry*, Englewood Cliffs, N.J., Prentice-Hall, 1966 (*in production*). Further information on NMR spectra may be found in J. D. Roberts, *Nuclear Magnetic Resonance*, New York, McGraw-Hill, 1959. Infrared, ultraviolet, and NMR spectra are dis-cussed in J. R. Dyer, *Applications of Absorption Spectroscopy of Organic Com-pounds*, Englewood Cliffs, N.J., Prentice-Hall, 1965, and in R. M. Silverstein and G. C. Bassler, *Spectrometric Identification of Organic Compounds*, New York, Wiley, 1963.

6

Rotational Isomerism

Up to this point we have assumed that rotation about single bonds was free, so that, for example, one of the methyl groups in ethane could rotate with respect to the other without any change in the energy of the molecule. In 1935 in England, E. Teller and B. Topley noted that the heat capacity of ethane was significantly lower than theory indicated that it should be, assuming free rotation. They suggested that if the rotation about the C—C bond were not free, but were hindered by an energy barrier, theory and experiment could be brought into agreement. Subsequent studies have shown that energy barriers to rotation exist for C—C bonds in general, as well as for C—N, C—O, and most other single bonds. Thus, the possibility of the existence of isomers that differed only in their internal rotational arrangements had to be considered, and this kind of isomerization was given some attention by a few chemists during the period from 1935 to 1950. Many of the basic principles involved were worked out during that period by physical chemists, the most notable contributions being made by K. S. Pitzer and his collaborators at the University of California.

6.1 CONFORMATIONAL ANALYSIS

In 1950 D. H. R. Barton (then at Glasgow) showed that many of the relative chemical and physical properties of complicated molecules could be formulated in terms of the rotational, or "conformational," arrangements present within the system. Molecules which differ from one another only by rotations about single bonds are said to be *conformational isomers*, or *conformers*. The interpretation of the properties of compounds in terms of conformations is referred to as *conformational analysis*. This is a branch of organic chemistry that is currently being explored by a number of chemists, and the fundamental ideas are now very clearly understood.[†]

[†] The difference between *conformation* and *configuration* is most easily seen by recognizing that to change conformation only a rotation about a single bond is required, while to change configuration requires the breaking of a bond, and re-forming it to give a new compound.

Returning to the rotational barrier in ethane, we can imagine two extremes in the rotational arrangement about the C—C bond; these are referred to as *eclipsed* and *staggered* arrangements. Both the perspective formulas and the Newman projections (end-on views) are shown for each:

eclipsed   staggered

eclipsed   staggered

The angle in the plane of the paper between a hydrogen on the nearer carbon and a hydrogen on the farther carbon in the Newman projection (the dihedral angle, ϕ) varies from 0° to 360° as one methyl rotates with respect to the other. If we take 0° as the eclipsed arrangement, then 60° corresponds to the staggered arrangement, and 120° is another eclipsed arrangement, and so on. The variation in energy with ϕ is an approximately sinusoidal curve, with three maxima and three minima. The height of this barrier in ethane is known to be 2.8 kcal/mole, and the data are summarized pictorially in Fig. 6-1. This barrier height is such that at

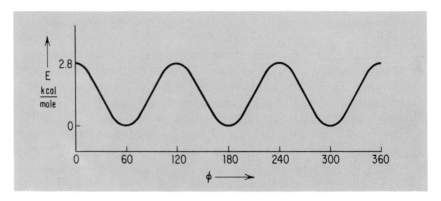

Fig. 6-1 The rotational energy of ethane.

room temperature the molecules are just rocking back and forth in the potential well most of the time, and only occasionally does one acquire enough energy to go "over the top." Things happen very rapidly on a molecular scale, however, and "only occasionally" still means many times per second. Conformers[†] are not usually isomers which can be separated and put in bottles; they exist as equilibrium mixtures.

Rotational barriers have been known to exist since 1936, but in spite of a very considerable amount of work since that time, we are still not really sure what causes them. A whole variety of reasons have alternately been put forth and disproven since that time. One simple picture was that the hydrogens are too close together in the eclipsed form, and a van der Waals repulsion exists between them; the repulsion was calculated to be only a tenth as large as that observed, however. Since the other explanations have also been disproven, one is led to ask whether a simple physical picture of the barrier can, in fact, be given. In any event, as incomplete as our understanding of such barriers may be, we know where they are and how large they are, and this is sufficient for us to make effective use of them in conformational analysis.

Examining one of the more complicated molecules n-butane, we see some features besides those previously discussed. If we consider the rotation about the central bond, we may expect a sinusoidal barrier similar to that in ethane. Furthermore, if the two methyls are eclipsing each

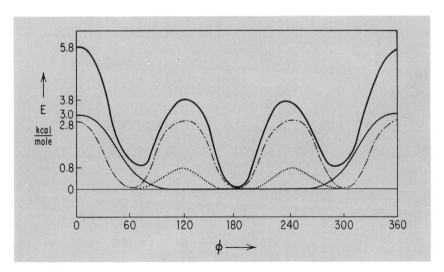

Fig. 6-2 The rotational energy of butane: total energy, ——; CH_3/CH_3 repulsion, ——; CH_3/H repulsion, ······; ethane barrier, –·–·–.

[†]This term is usually restricted to conformational arrangements that correspond to energy minima.

other, they are each well within the van der Waals radius of the other. This additional van der Waals repulsion amounts to about 3 kcal/mole at $\phi = 0°$, drops to about 0.8 kcal/mole at $\phi = 60°$, and continues to drop, reaching zero at approximately $\phi = 120°$. At this last angle the methyls are each a little too close to their respective eclipsed hydrogens, and the sum of this pair of resulting van der Waals repulsions amounts to about 1 kcal/mole. This repulsion sum falls to zero by the time ϕ increases (or decreases) by 60°. The components which contribute to the rotational energy of *n*-butane may, then, be pictured as in Fig. 6-2, their sum giving the resultant curve. For most purposes we are interested in the energy minima, since these correspond to the conformations which the molecules will ordinarily have. It can be seen that in the case of *n*-butane the minimum of lowest energy is at $\phi = 180°$, and the other two minima are about 0.8 kcal/mole higher than that. The first arrangement is called the *anti*, or *trans* conformation, and the less favorable minima are called *gauche* conformations (the two *gauche* conformations are enantiomers of each other); *n*-butane, then, exists as a mixture of *anti* and *gauche* conformers, the former being the more stable and the major component of the mixture:

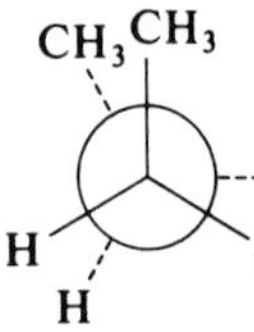

0°

eclipsed

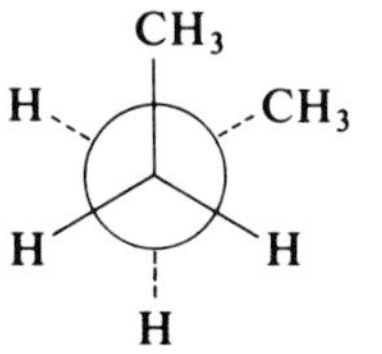

60°

gauche

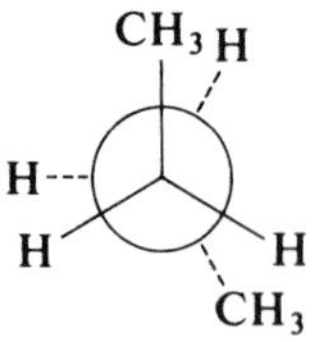

120°

eclipsed

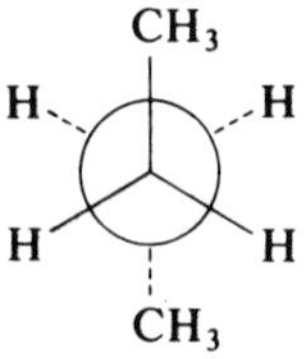

180°

anti

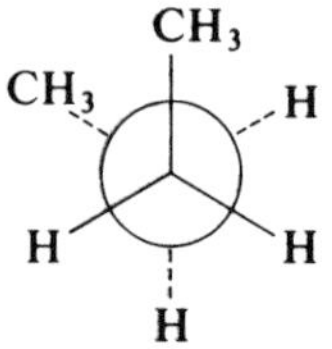

300°

gauche

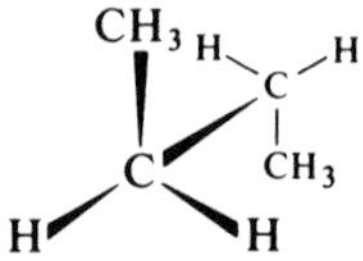

anti

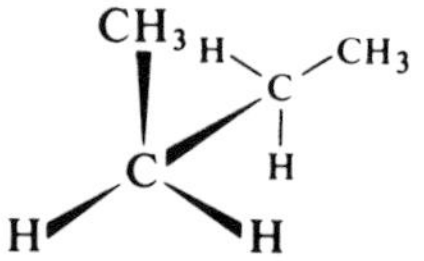

gauche

The *n*-alkanes exist as completely *anti* chains in crystals:

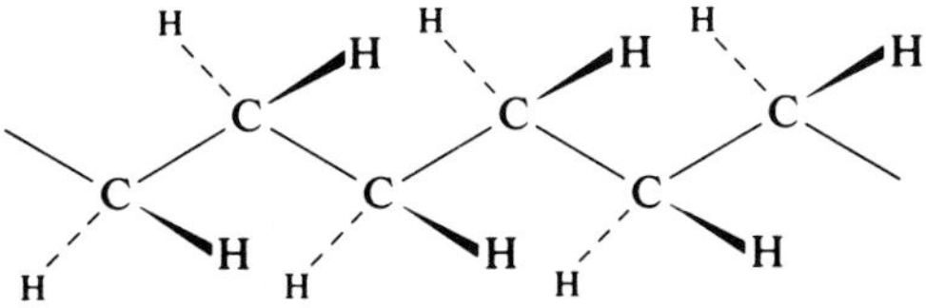

anti conformation of an alkane

In the liquid phase, however, there are a significant number of molecules which are *gauche* at any one bond at a given instant, and fewer which are *gauche* at two bonds (in different possible combinations), and fewer yet which are *gauche* at three bonds, and so on. The alkanes, then, if they are very large, are usually mixtures of a great number of conformers, and their conformational properties are consequently somewhat hard to study.

One special case of restricted rotation about a single bond was recognized in the 1920's; it concerned *ortho*-substituted biphenyls. Simple biphenyl derivatives tend to be nearly planar (because of the conjugation energy) but the rotation about the central bond is nearly free:

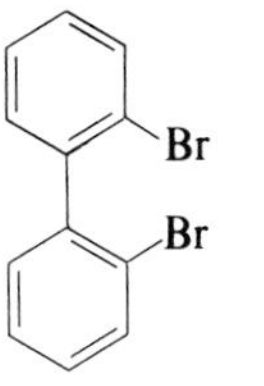

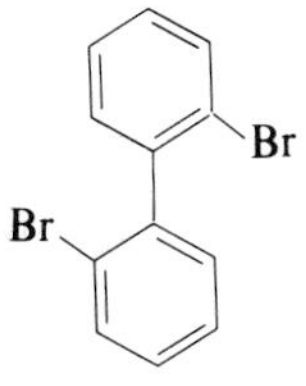

If there are four bulky *ortho* substituents, as in 2,2'-dinitro-2,2'-dicarboxy-biphenyl, it is not possible for the molecule to have the two aromatic rings coplanar because of the repulsion between the *ortho* substituents. Two nonplanar forms for this molecule are shown, which are in fact mirror images:

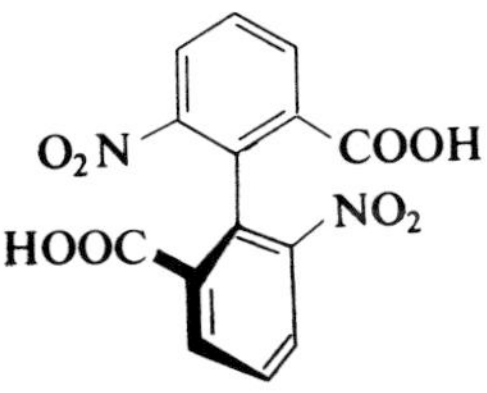

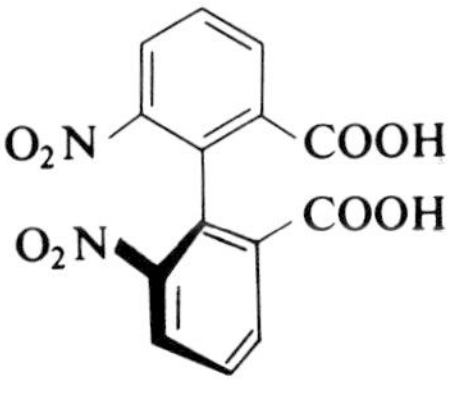

The molecules are asymmetric even though they do not contain asymmetric atoms, and they show optical activity for reasons analogous to those given for the allenes (Sec. 4.3). Some biphenyls (with large *ortho* substituents) are optically stable, others are stable at room temperature but racemized on heating, and still others (with small substituents) are racemized so easily that they are not resolvable (separable into enantio-mers).

6.2 CYCLOHEXANE SYSTEMS

We tend to think of the alkanes as "simple cases" for most purposes but, as far as conformational properties are concerned, this is not so. The most simple system from a conformational point of view is cyclo-hexane. The most stable conformer of this molecule is the so-called chair form. This conformer is rigid in the sense that to change the dihedral angle about any bond or bonds requires a simultaneous change in one or more of the C—C—C bond angles in the molecule. Such a deformation costs a considerable amount of energy, so the molecule is effectively held in a potential well about 10 kcal/mole in depth.

From the point of view of conformational analysis, the cyclohexane ring is particularly simple because of two facts: first, there is a single con-formation (less than 1% of other conformations at room temperature) and, second, the molecule has a high degree of symmetry. The symmetry is such that the hydrogens can be divided into two kinds only, which are called *axial* and *equatorial*.

cyclohexane   axial hydrogens   equatorial hydrogens

The axial C—H bonds are all parallel to one another and to the sym-metry axis of the molecule, which is shown passing vertically through the center of the ring. As we proceed around the ring, one axial hydrogen points up, the next points down, the next up, and so on. The equatorial hydrogens all lie approximately in the plane of the ring, and also alternate in their up-down directions. If the axial hydrogen on a given carbon points straight up, the equatorial hydrogen on the same carbon points slightly down, and vice versa. The chair form of cyclohexane can deform itself into another high-energy structure, commonly referred to as a boat form, from which it can go back to the original chair. Alternatively, it can invert to give another chair, in which the hydrogens that were originally axial have now become equatorial and vice versa. Since in cyclohexane there are only two conformational types of hydrogen, in a monosubstituted cyclohexane such as methylcyclohexane there exists an equilibrium in which only two conformations are present to a significant extent, and these are two chair forms, one with the methyl group axial and the other with it equatorial. Since methylcyclohexane is a mixture of the two conformers in rapid equilibrium, we can ask which conformer is the more stable and by how much.

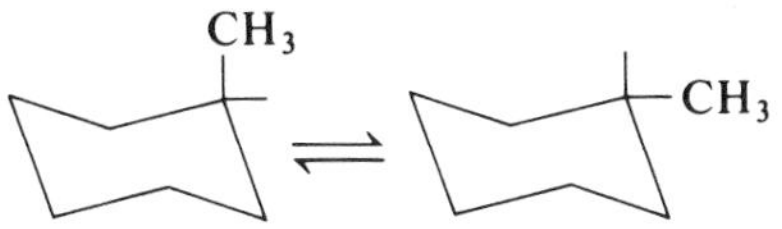

axial
methylcyclohexane

equatorial
methylcyclohexane

We can, in fact, analyze the molecule in terms of the number of butane units that have the *anti* arrangement in one conformation and the *gauche* arrangement in the other. As with *n*-butane itself, each *gauche* conformation might be expected to increase the energy of the molecule 0.8 kcal/mole above that of the corresponding *anti* conformation, and in fact the best experimental value for the number is 0.85 kcal/mole. Any interaction that involves only atoms of the ring will be the same in either conformation, so these need not be considered. We need look only at those interactions which involve the methyl, and there are two of these for each conformation. If the methyl is equatorial, these interactions are both *anti;* if it is axial, they are both *gauche:*

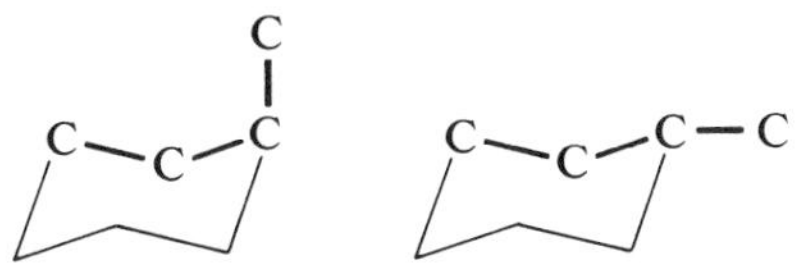

gauche interaction   *anti* interaction

This means that the equatorial conformer is more stable than the axial by 1.7 kcal/mole, and at room temperature it therefore will comprise about 95% of the equilibrium mixture.

The conformational properties of the methyl group become of greater chemical importance in disubstituted cyclohexane systems. In 1,4-dimethylcyclohexane, for example, the *trans* isomer[†] is a mixture of two conformations, diequatorial and diaxial, the former being the more stable:

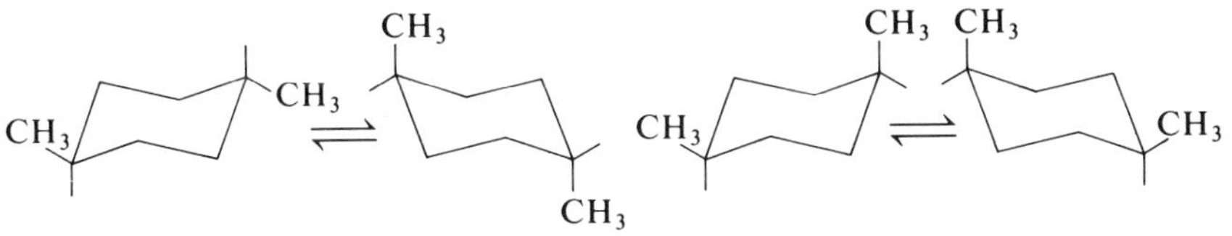

E	0		3.4	1.7		1.7
(kcal/mole):	*trans*				*cis*	

[†] In cyclic systems, the ring is projected onto an average plane, and if any two substituents are on the same side of the plane they are said to be *cis*, and if on opposite sides they are *trans*. Thus *trans*-1,4-dimethylcyclohexane has the methyls on opposite sides of the mean plane in both conformations.

The *cis* isomer is a single conformation, because inversion to the other chair gives a conformation indistinguishable from the original one. The diequatorial conformer is also more stable than the *cis* isomer by 1.7 kcal/mole.[†] With the 1,3-dimethylcyclohexanes, the most stable conformation is found to be the diequatorial form of the *cis* isomer, the *trans* isomer having the less favorable equatorial-axial arrangement:

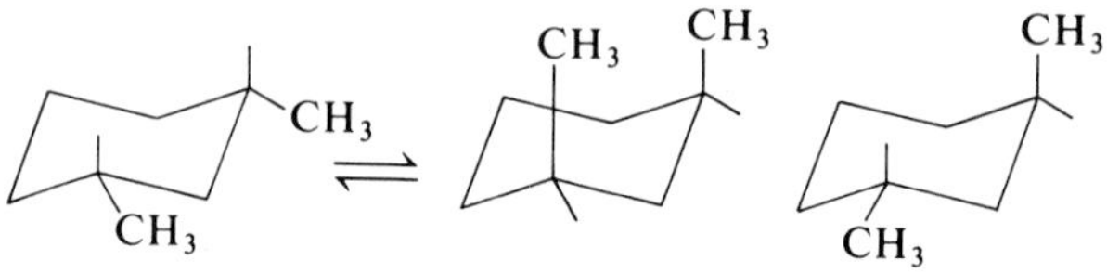

E (kcal/mole):   0   large   1.7

                     cis   *trans*

The 1,2-dimethylcyclohexanes are a little more complicated because the two methyls are here sufficiently close that they can interact with one another. Again, the diequatorial conformation of the *trans* isomer is the most stable.

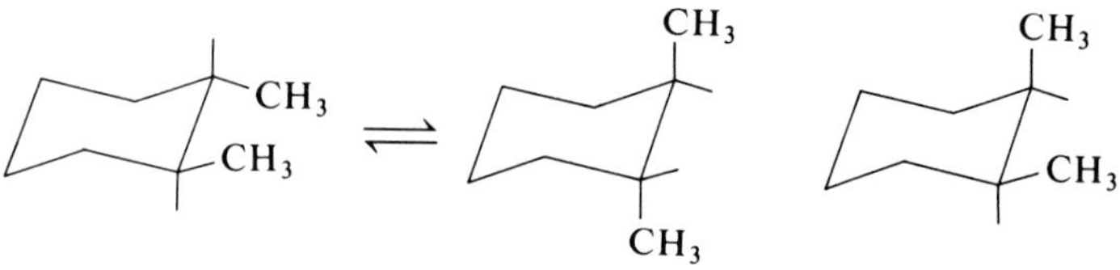

E (kcal/mole):   0.85   3.4   2.55

                     trans   *cis*

The greater stability of an isomer with equatorial substituents is quite general. The most common hexose (β-D-glucose) is the diastereomer in which all of the substituents are equatorial:

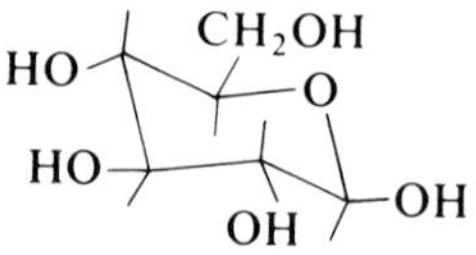

The relative stabilities of fused systems of such cyclohexane rings as decalin (decahydronapthalene) are easily understood in terms of *gauche* interactions:

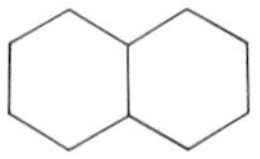

decalin

[†] Such values are found experimentally from heat-of-combustion measurements or from measurements of the positions of equilibria between isomers where the isomers are actually separable. Sometimes conformational equilibria can be measured (even though isolation of the individual conformers is not possible) by using physical methods, such as spectra.

To find the difference in the stabilities of the *cis* and *trans* isomers it is only necessary to know the difference between the number of *gauche* interactions in each isomer. We need only count those interactions that differ in the two isomers, which means those interactions that involve both rings simultaneously. In *trans*-decalin the pertinent interactions involve the sequences 2-1-9-8, 1-9-8-7, 3-4-10-5, 4-10-5-6, 1-9-10-5, 8-9-10-4:

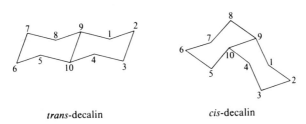

trans-decalin   cis-decalin

Each sequence can be seen to correspond to an *anti* butane segment. In the *cis* isomer the first, fourth, and sixth sequences correspond to *anti*, the others to *gauche*, butane segments. The *cis* isomer therefore has a predicted energy that is $3 \times 0.85 = 2.55$ kcal/mole higher than the *trans*, and this is what is found experimentally.

Larger systems, such as the perhydroanthracenes, can be treated in a similar manner:

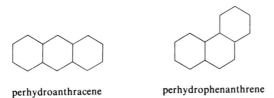

perhydroanthracene   perhydrophenanthrene

If larger alkyl groups, such as ethyl or isopropyl, are placed on the cyclohexane ring, the equatorial conformation is more stable than the axial by an amount similar to that found in methyl. With isopropyl, for example, there are two *gauche* interactions between the equatorial isopropyl group and the ring in the most favorable conformation, whereas there are four if the group is axial, and the difference in conformational energies is calculated to be 1.7 kcal/mole, just as in the case of methyl. Actually, the axial isopropyl is more constrained than the corresponding methyl, since only the conformation in which both the methyls are away from the ring is really possible (the conformation with one methyl back

Table 6-1

THE CONFORMATIONAL ENERGIES OF
VARIOUS GROUPS

Group	Energy (kcal/mole)
methyl	1.7
ethyl	1.8
isopropyl	2.0
tert-butyl	>5
—F	0.3
—Cl	0.4
—Br	0.4
—OH	0.6

over the ring would have a severe interaction between the ring and the methyl, and the energy actually would be too high for the conformation to exist). The equatorial isopropyl, on the other hand, has three conformations which do not differ greatly in energy. The axial isopropyl is therefore slightly less favorable with respect to the equatorial than is the methyl. The conformational energies of a number of common groups are given in Table 6-1. The *tert*-butyl group is seen to be in quite a different class from most of the other alkyl groups; it is of such a nature that, when axial, it would necessarily have one methyl group pointing into the ring:

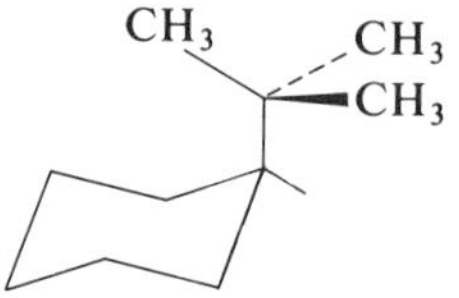

The van der Waals repulsion between that methyl and the two methylenes (C-3 and C-5) is greater than 5 kcal/mole. This energy is so large that to avoid it the ring adopts another geometry altogether, called the boat form. Thus, *trans*-1,3-di-*tert*-butylcyclohexane, in which one *tert*-butyl would have to be axial in the chair form, exists largely in the boat form, both its groups in positions which are equatorial-like:

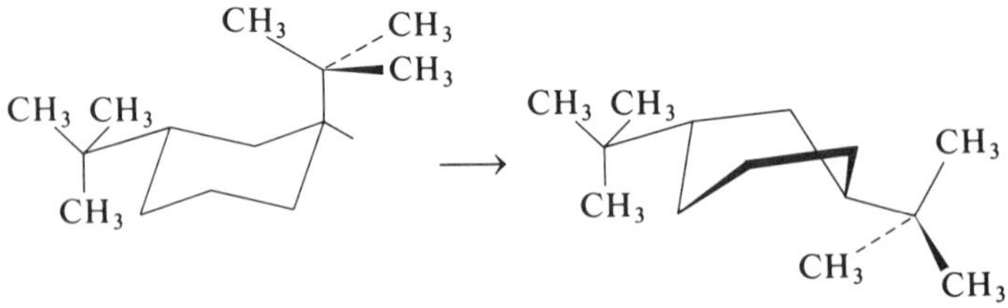

The possibility of the existence of a boat form for cyclohexane was recognized as long ago as 1890. It has natural (tetrahedral) bond angles, as does the chair, and these are the only two forms which do. The boat is not rigid, however, and can flex into what is referred to as a stretched form without any bond angle deformation:

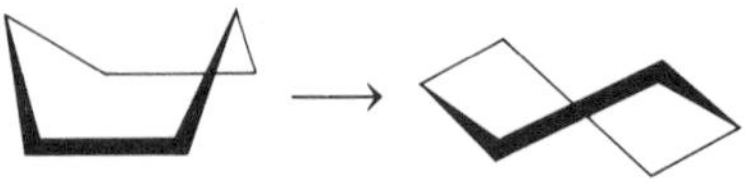

By a continuous flexing motion the prow (or stern) of the boat moves around the ring, from C-1 to C-2 to C-3, etc. This motion has led to the boat form being referred to as the *flexible form*. Boat forms are found to be of much higher energy than chair forms in simple cases. The symmetrical boat clearly contains two eclipsed ethane units, whereas in the chair form all of the ethane segments are staggered. Two of the dihedral angles in the stretched form are more favorable than those which are eclipsed in the regular boat, but the other four are less favorable. The result is that the total energies of the regular boat and stretched forms are similar. The boat might thus be estimated to have some 5.6 kcal/mole more energy than the chair (twice the eclipsing energy of ethane), and experimental values near that number have been measured.[†]

To invert the cyclohexane ring, as is required if the equatorial methylcyclohexane is to be converted to the axial conformer, it is necessary that the molecule go through the flexible form. To go from the chair to the flexible form requires both eclipsing and angular deformation, and the energy barrier to this conversion is 10 kcal/mole. A complete *reaction coordinate diagram* for the change is shown in Fig. 6-3.

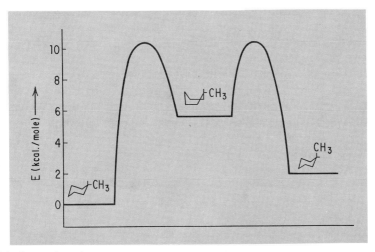

Fig. 6-3 Conversion of equatorial to axial methylcyclohexane.

If we have a single polar substituent, such as an —OH group, on a cyclohexane ring, or one polar substituent and one or more nonpolar ones, the conformational problems are fundamentally the same as those with the mono- or polyalkylcyclohexanes. If there are two or more polar groups, there is an electrostatic interaction between the groups, in addi-

---

[†]The energy of the classical boat form might be expected to be somewhat higher than this, since it actually corredponds more nearly to two eclipsed butanes. The most stable arrangement of the flexible form appears to be, not this classical boat, but the form shown in the figure, which is sometimes referred to as a "stretched" or "twisted" boat. From the dihedral angles of this form and the curve in Fig. 6-2, the quoted value is estimated.

tion to the various usual steric interactions.   The *trans* isomer of 1,2-dibromocyclohexane will illustrate this effect:

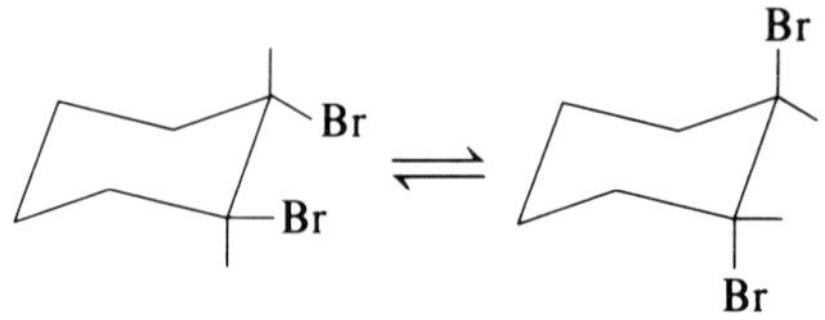

The conformational energy of an axial bromine is 0.4 kcal/mole; hence, since the two bromines do not overlap their van der Waals radii, we might guess that the diequatorial conformation would be more stable than the diaxial by 0.8 kcal/mole.   Actually, it is found that in benzene solution there are equal amounts of the two conformations; hence, they are of equal energy.   There must be an additional interaction energy involved, which just balances the 0.8 kcal/mole of steric repulsion energy present in the diaxial form.   When we consider the C—Br bonds as dipoles, we can see that it is electrostatically more favorable to have the negative ends of the dipoles as far apart as possible (diaxial), and the electrostatic repulsion in this conformation must, in fact, be less by 0.8 kcal/mole than in the diequatorial conformation.

There are various physical and chemical differences in properties of a given group, depending on whether it is axial or equatorial.   A group's stretching frequency in the infrared spectrum, for example, is typically higher for an equatorial substituent than for its axial counterpart:

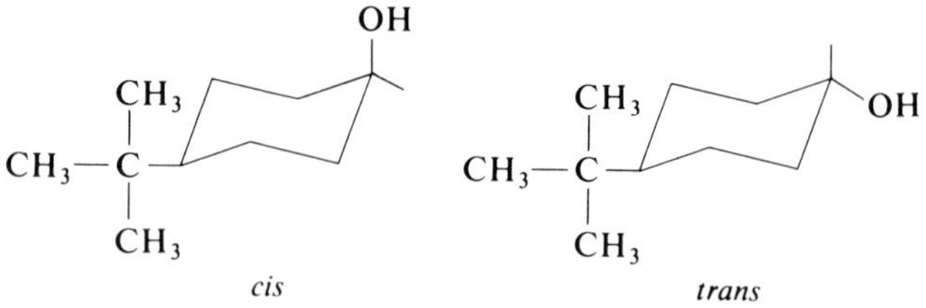

The *cis*- and *trans*-4-*tert*-butylcyclohexanols have their hydroxyls held effectively in axial and equatorial positions, and the C—O stretching vibrations are found at 955 and 1062 cm^{-1}, respectively, in accord with the general rule.   These bands can be used to assign conformation (and hence configuration, usually) in various systems, and have been used for quantitative measurements of equilibria.

6.3 OTHER RING SYSTEMS

Since the interior angles of a regular pentagon (108°) are nearly those of a tetrahedron, it was long assumed that cyclopentane had a planar arrangement of its carbon atoms.   In a planar form, however, each pair of carbons has an energetically unfavorable, eclipsed arrangement. If one or two of the carbons were to move a little way out of the plane of the others, at least some of the dihedral angles could be substantially improved, but at the cost of compressing some of the C—C—C bond angles to less than 108°. A compromise between these interactions is reached, and cyclopentane is, in fact, slightly nonplanar. The nonplanarity rotates around the ring, in a manner similar to that displayed by the flexible form of cyclohexane. Even cyclobutane has been found to be nonplanar for the same reason. The conformational properties of cyclopentane have been studied much less thoroughly than those of cyclohexane, because there are at least six nonequivalent positions on the cyclopentane ring, and the conformational problem is much more involved. The same difficulties exist with rings larger than cyclohexane.

The rings containing 3 or 4 members are usually referred to as small rings, the 5-to-7-membered ones as common rings, the 8-to-12-membered ones as medium rings, and those containing more than 12 ring atoms as large, or macro, rings. The large rings present no special structural features, but the medium rings do have properties that set them apart from the others. The medium rings are noteworthy for their relative instability, as indicated by their large heats of combustion (Table 6-2), and for the difficulty encountered in trying to close acyclic chains to form them, which again indicates an instability. The reason for this instability becomes apparent when it is recognized that in a regular symmetrical crown structure, as that of cyclohexane or cyclooctane as pictured,

Table 6-2

HEATS OF COMBUSTION OF CYCLOALKANES $(CH_2)_n$ PER METHYLENE GROUP[†]

n	H.C./n	n	H.C./n
3	166.6	8	158.6
4	163.9	9	158.8
5	158.7	10	158.6
6	157.4	12	157.7
7	158.3	14	157.4

[†]In kilocalories per mole of the cycloalkane in the gas phase, divided by the number of methylene groups.

the dihedral angles are not independent variables but are fixed for a given set of bond angles. In these regular crowns the dihedral angles are such that, in the case of cyclohexane, there is little torsional strain, the ethane units all lying at torsional minima of energy. In an eight-membered ring, the torsional energy is very sizeable, it is worse in the ten-membered ring, and becomes progressively better in the twelve-membered and larger rings. Actually the molecules undergo various kinds of deformations so as to decrease their total energy. Cyclooctane, for example, does not have the symmetrical crown structure, but is distorted somewhat. This distortion makes some of the dihedral angles energetically better and some worse, but the overall energy of the molecule is lower. Cyclodecane expands the

C—C—C bond angles by various amounts up to 118°, and in so doing is able to reduce greatly its torsional energy at the expense of only a moderate amount of bending energy. These medium rings are found to have positions which are approximately equatorial and others which are approximately axial, but there are different kinds of each. The conformational problems here are formidable indeed, and so far very little progress has been made in their solution.

6.4 PROTEINS

The primary structures of proteins and peptides were discussed in Chap. 5, and while their determination is exceedingly difficult, it has been accomplished in a number of cases. Once the primary structure of the protein is known we are faced with a problem which in many ways is even more difficult, and that is to determine the actual three-dimensional structure of the protein. Very few of the techniques applicable to the determination of conformational structures of small molecules are useful for proteins. The infrared spectrum, for example, shows such a jumble of smeared-out bands as to be utterly uninformative, and the same is true of most other methods. The only method which shows promise for the complete elucidation of the three-dimensional structure of a protein is x-ray crystallography. An x-ray diffraction pattern of a crystalline protein shows many thousands of reflections, the intensity and spacing of each of which must be individually measured. It is then possible in principle to determine the structure which gave rise to this diffraction pattern, but the mathematical calculations required are exceedingly complicated. The fundamental unit of structure in almost all of the proteins appears, from x-ray diffraction studies and other methods, to be the so-called α-helix. The helical conformation for proteins was suggested on logical grounds before it was established experimentally. While a paraffin hydrocarbon tends to extend itself in a zigzag fashion in order to minimize the repulsion between its various parts, a polar molecule such as a protein finds itself in quite a different energetical situation. As the electrostatic effects between the various dipoles in the molecule are very large, the whole protein will tend to orient itself in such a way as to minimize the total electrostatic energy. This means that the positive end of one dipole will try to be next to the negative end of another, and so on throughout the molecule. The hydrogen on nitrogen is quite positive, while the oxygen is quite negative, and there is a strong tendency to form a *hydrogen bond* (really an electrostatic bond) of the form —N—H . . . O= wherever possible. To maintain effective resonance, it is essential that the nitrogen and the carbonyl and all of their attached groups be nearly coplanar. In addition, it is desirable to have a structure in which the polar groups are on the surface, available for interaction with the solvent and with one another, while the nonpolar groups also are together to avoid interfering with the interactions between the polar groups. A structure that satisfies all these requirements is the α-helix (Fig. 6-4). There are 3.6 amino acid residues per turn of the helix and, just as all amino acids in proteins are of the same (L) configuration, so all protein helices are right-handed, as illustrated.

Most proteins are very compact structures, and most belong to the group referred to as globular proteins. The globular shape is not consistent with a simple single helix, but requires that the helix be bent and folded back on itself. This bending and folding of the protein is referred to as its *tertiary* structure. Just why proteins choose to adopt the specific tertiary structures they do is not clear at the present time. It appears that a given primary structure will have a natural tendency to assume the specific secondary and tertiary structures that are found. The tertiary structure determined by the x-ray method, of course, applies to the protein in the crystal. We are, however, really interested in the structure in solution, where the protein ordinarily is found and functions, and where, hopefully, the tertiary structure is the same as in the crystal.

Proteins are rather delicate compounds as far as their biological activity is concerned. Exposure to acid, base, heat, or other materials leads more or less easily to a loss of the biological activity, concurrent with changes in the tertiary structure. In general, the exact shape of a protein must not be altered, if it is to perform its intended function; the substrate with which the protein is to react fits onto or into the protein as a key fits a lock, and even a small conformational change may render the protein biologically useless. For this reason only one enantiomer of a substrate usually will react with enzymatic catalysis.

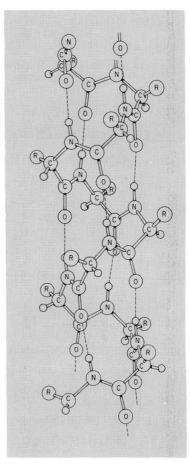

Fig. 6-4. The helical structure of a portion of a typical globular protein. (From *The Nature of the Chemical Bond*, by L. Pauling, third edition, Copyright, 1960, by Cornell University; used with the permission of Cornell University Press).

A typical globular protein whose tertiary structure is now fairly well established is myoglobin. It contains a single polypeptide chain coiled in a very compact way. There are eight nonhelical regions in the molecule; the portions shown as tubular in Fig. 6-5 are for the most part helical. At this writing only this general form of the myoglobin molecule is known.

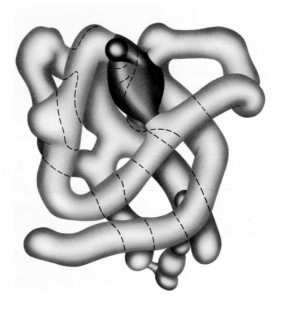

Fig. 6-5 The tertiary structure of myoglobin. (Courtesy of Dr. John C. Kendrew.)

The structures of proteins are obviously exceedingly complicated, and our understanding of them is vague and incomplete. This is an area in which much research is being done, and which chemists find as exciting as it is difficult.

6.5 STERIC INHIBITION OF RESONANCE

The orbital pictures of molecules containing conjugated systems show clearly that rotation of the system from planarity will disrupt the conjugation. There are a large number of examples of compounds in which this effect has been detected experimentally. In Sec. 5.7, the resonance between amino or nitro groups and an attached aromatic ring was noted. The compound N, N-dimethyl-p-nitroaniline has a moment of 6.87 D, which is larger than that calculated from addition of the group dipole moments, and which results from the continuous nature of the conjugation:

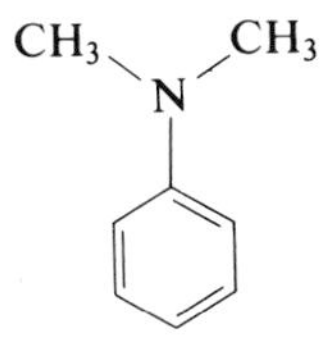

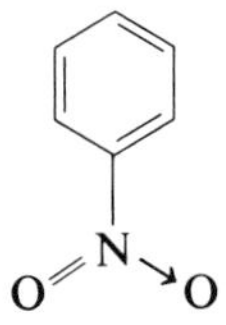

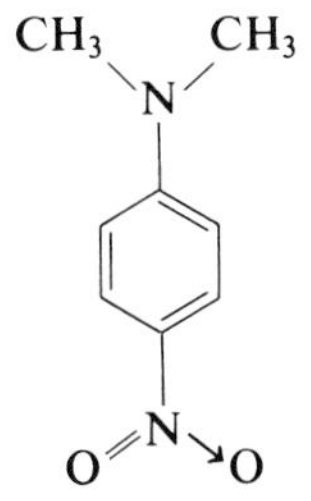

1.58 D   3.95 D   6.87 D

Durene (1,2,4,5-tetramethylbenzene) has no dipole moment, for reasons of symmetry. One might be led to suppose that nitrodimethylamino-durene would also have a moment of 6.87 D; in fact, it has a moment considerably less than the vector sum of the nitro and dimethylamino dipoles:

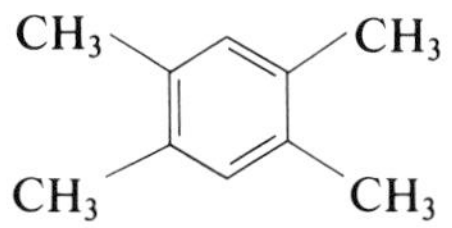

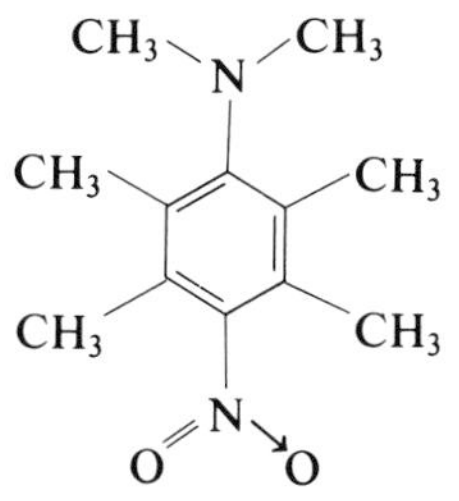

0 D   4.11 D

Thus, not only is the resonance interaction between the two groups supressed, but the resonance interaction of each of these groups with the ring has also been decreased. The reason for these results is that the bulky methyl groups on the aromatic ring interfere with the coplanarity of the

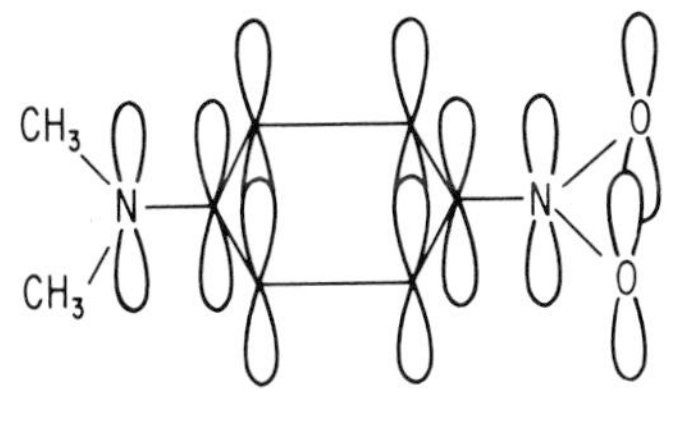

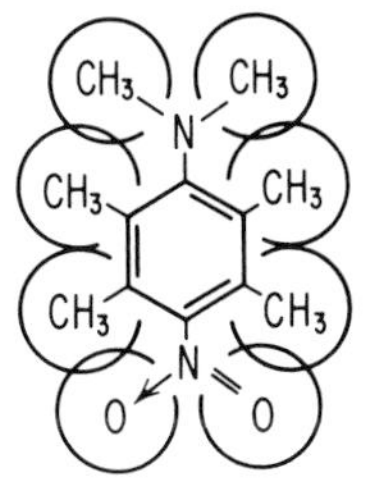

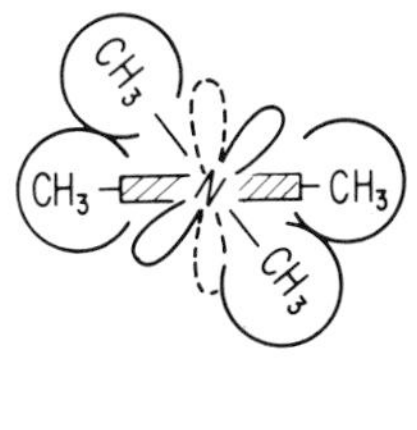

π system, as indicated in the figure. The result is that the overlap between the π orbitals of the ring and the nitrogen atoms is decreased and the resonance is not very effective.

6.6 PROBLEMS

1. Draw all the conformations (chair forms) for each isomer of 1,3,5-trimethylcyclohexane and calculate their conformational energies.

2. Which is the more stable and by how much: *cis*- or *trans*-9-methyldecalin?

3. Why are the medium rings strained? Compare with the small rings.

4. *p*-Nitrotoluene (*p*-nitromethylbenzene) is approximately as acidic as phenol, while 2,4,6-trimethylnitrobenzene is hardly acidic at all. Explain.

5. Compare the preferred conformational arrangements in hydrocarbons and in proteins. Explain.

SUGGESTED READINGS

The title subject is discussed in detail in E. L. Eliel, N. L. Allinger, S. J. Angyal, and G. B. Morrison, *Conformational Analysis*, New York, Wiley, 1965. A less detailed coverage of the subject is given in E. L. Eliel, *Stereochemistry of Carbon Compounds*, New York, McGraw-Hill, 1962.

Chemical Reaction Intermediates

There are many compounds or intermediates which occur momentarily during the course of chemical reactions; these are of interest, but usually are not sufficiently stable to be isolated. There are four simple types of intermediates that carbon may form; they are the carbonium ion, the carbanion, the free radical and the carbene:

$CH_3^{\oplus}$	$CH_3^{\ominus}$	CH_3	$:CH_2$
methyl carbonium ion	methyl carbanion	methyl radical	carbene

The structures of the first two of these can be rather well predicted by analogy with trimethyl boron and ammonia, respectively, with which they are *isoelectronic* (have the same electron structure). The carbonium ion is found to be planar, like the boron compound and for the same reasons (Sec. 5.2). The carbanion is pyramidal but easily inverted, analogous to ammonia. The geometries of the other two species are more difficult to predict, and they are also less clear experimentally. It appears that carbon radicals are planar or else very easily inverted pyramids. The carbene must have an empty p orbital, and something near sp^2 hybridization for the other three carbon orbitals, and there is probably substantially greater s character in the lone-pair orbital than in the bonding orbitals and, hence, an H—C—H bond angle of somewhat less than 120°. The geometries of the intermediates are chemically important because, if a planar intermediate such as a carbonium ion exists in a chemical reaction, a pure enantiomer may be converted, via such a symmetrical intermediate, to a racemic product:

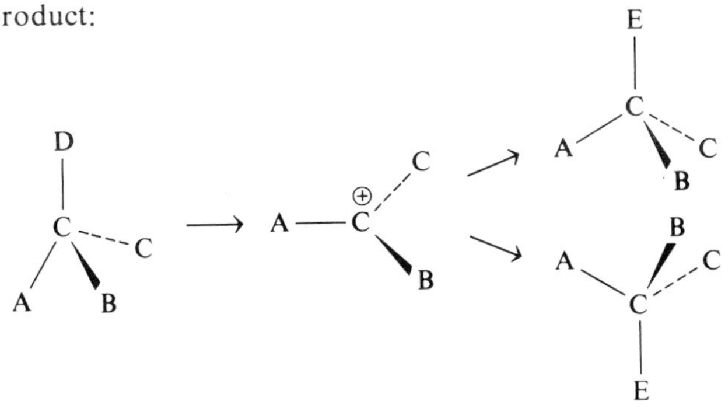

When only pyramidal or tetrahedral intermediates exist in a reaction, a reactant which is a pure enantiomer can be converted to a product which is also a pure enantiomer.

Of these various chemical intermediates, the carbonium ion is the best understood, and we may consider it in some detail. The *tert*-butylcarbonium ion, $(CH_3)_3C^{\oplus}$, while not sufficiently stable to be isolated, is at least stable enough to have a transitory existence. The corresponding methyl carbonium ion, $CH_3^{\oplus}$, has never been demonstrated to exist in chemical reactions, even momentarily. There are at least two reasons why the *tert*-butylcarbonium ion is very much more stable than the methyl carbonium ion.

The first reason for this is due to the inductive effect of the methyl groups. A C—C bond is more polarizable than a C—H bond, which means that it is more subject to deformation by the application of a force. A positive charge in the molecule is a force and, as a result of its presence, the electron pairs forming the σ bonds will be pulled toward the positive center and no longer shared as evenly as in a neutral hydrocarbon. The force is more effective in pulling in the surrounding electrons from a C—C bond than from a C—H bond,[†] the charge is more delocalized in the first case, and the resulting ion is more stable.

The second reason for the greater stability of the *tert*-butylcarbonium ion is *hyperconjugation*. One can write the following resonance forms when there are alkyl groups attached to the ionic carbon:

$$CH_3\!-\!\overset{\oplus}{\underset{\underset{CH_3}{|}}{C}}\!-\!CH_3 \longleftrightarrow H\!-\!\overset{\overset{H}{|}}{C}\!=\!\overset{}{\underset{\underset{\underset{\oplus H}{CH_3}}{|}}{C}}\!-\!CH_3$$

(9 forms)

Here the nine hyperconjugative resonance forms do not involve charge separation, but they are not very favorable because they require generation of a weak C—C π bond at the expense of a strong C—H σ bond. Any one such form contributes little to the resonance hybrid, but all nine of them exert a very marked stabilizing effect.

We have, then, an inductive effect and a hyperconjugative effect, both working together to make tertiary carbonium ions more stable than primary. Extending the argument outlined, it can be seen that the stability of a secondary ion is between those of the primary and tertiary ions.

If resonance forms of the Kekulé type are possible, the carbonium ion will be further stabilized. Thus, the allyl carbonium ion, a primary but resonance-stabilized ion, has a stability comparable to that of the *tert*-

---

[†]The outer, or bonding, electrons are generally farther from the nucleus, more loosely held, and more polarizable as the elements in which they exist are lower in the periodic table.

butyl ion:

$$\overset{\oplus}{CH=CH-CH_2} \longleftrightarrow \overset{\oplus}{CH_2}-CH=CH_2$$

Similarly, the benzyl ion is rather stable:

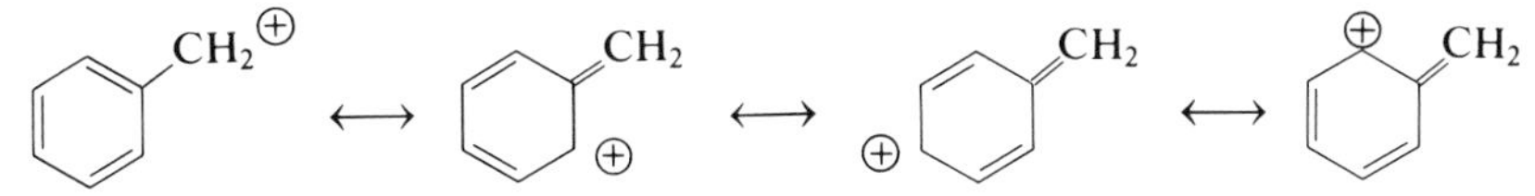

Similar resonance forms can be written for the corresponding radicals and anions, which are also found to be more stable than their simple aliphatic counterparts.

Compounds that can form enols can also form enolate ions upon treatment with a base, **B**:

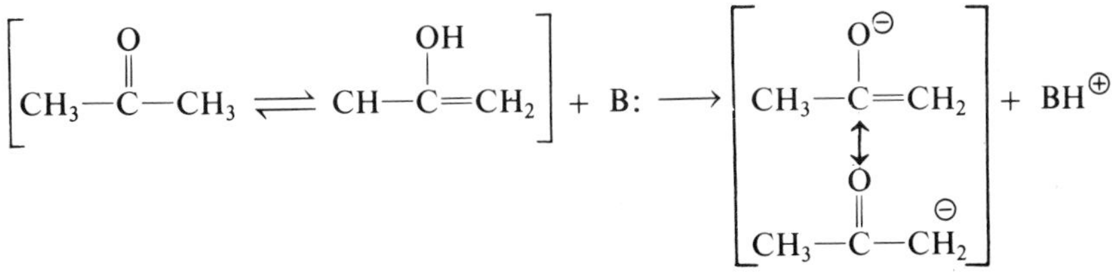

The enolate ion is resonance-stabilized, and compounds that can form such ions are weakly acidic, about like alcohols. Among such compounds are esters, ketones, aldehydes, nitriles, nitroparaffins, and many other structural types. The carbanion in these molecules is doubtlessly planar, as the unshared pair may then occupy a *p* orbital for effective resonance:

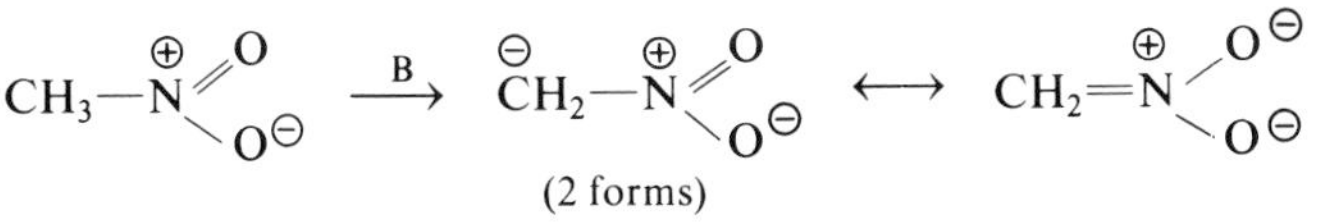

(2 forms)

If two or more powerful electron-withdrawing groups are attached to the same carbon, a proton on that carbon will be even more acidic—in the range of a phenol to carboxylic acid. Compounds of this type often have enol forms which are sufficiently stable to be isolable. Acetoacetic ester is such a compound. The keto and enol tautomers have each been separately prepared (on standing they slowly revert to an equilibrium mixture of the two):

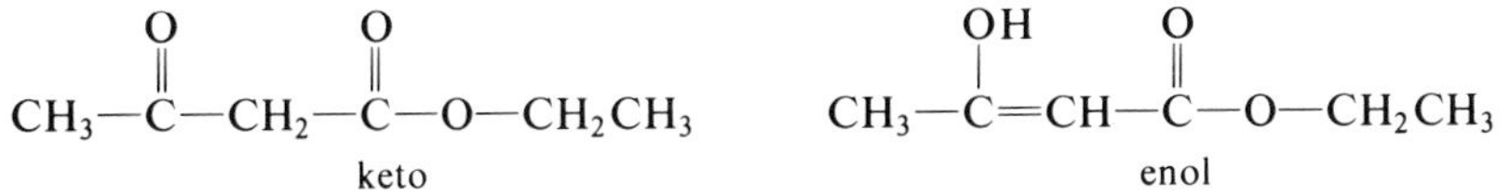

keto   enol

acetoacetic ester

The enol form in such a compound is stabilized by both conjugation of the enolic double bond with the carbonyl group and by hydrogen bonding of the hydroxyl with the carbonyl oxygen.

PROBLEMS

1. Write Lewis structures and draw orbital pictures for methyl carbonium ion, methyl carbanion, carbene, and the methyl radical.

2. Show (partly in terms of resonance forms) why the *tert*-butyl carbonium ion is more stable than the methyl carbonium ion. Would you expect this to be also true of the corresponding radicals? Why?

3. Draw the enol forms and the important resonance forms of the enolate ions for the following molecules:

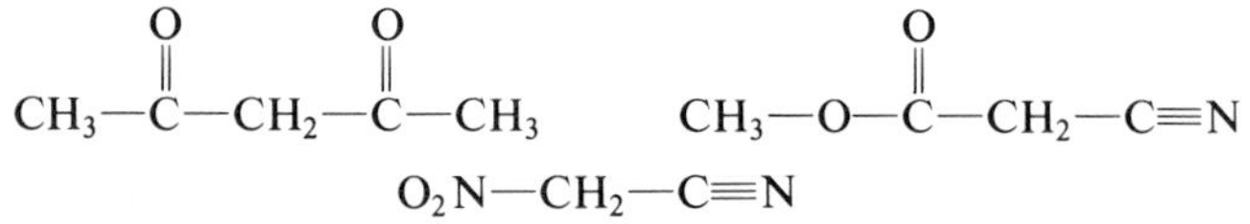

$$
\underset{\text{O}}{\overset{\text{O}}{\parallel}}\ \ \ \ \underset{\text{O}}{\overset{\text{O}}{\parallel}}
$$

$$
CH_3-C-CH_2-C-CH_3 \qquad CH_3-O-C-CH_2-C\equiv N
$$

$$
O_2N-CH_2-C\equiv N
$$

4. Compare the hybridization and geometry of the carbanions formed from propane and acetone.

SUGGESTED   READINGS

The chemical behavior of reaction intermediates is discussed in texts on reaction mechanisms; two such texts are: R. Stewart, *The Investigation of Organic Reactions*, Englewood Cliffs, N. J., Prentice-Hall, 1966 (*in production*), and E. S. Gould, *Mechanism and Structure in Organic Chemistry*, New York, Holt, Rinehart & Winston, 1959.

Chemical
Reactions

A chemical reaction is a process which converts one structure into another. A thorough understanding of a reaction requires first, that we know the structure of the material with which we start; second, that we know the structure of the material at the end of the reaction; and, finally, that we know, quantitatively, what happens in between these two states. The first six chapters of this book discussed the structures of compounds, the materials corresponding to the starting and product states. Chapter 7 covered the structures of the common reaction intermediates, or states of more or less stability which are formed and endure for some time during the course of a reaction. This chapter will be concerned with the processes involved in getting from one state to another state, the corresponding energy changes, the geometric requirements of the reaction, and the relationships between these things and structure.

For a reaction of the general type A $\rightarrow$ B, there are two aspects of the energetics to consider. We are interested, first, in the ratio B:A when the reaction goes to equilibrium (the *thermodynamics* of the reaction), and, second, in the rate at which this reaction occurs (the *kinetics* of the reaction).

8.1 THERMODYNAMICS

Suppose states A and B have energies E_1 and E_2, respectively, the latter being lower as in Fig. 8-1. A molecule going from A to B loses an amount of energy $\Delta E = (E_1 - E_2)$. If the molecule can move freely between A and B, there is a certain probability that it will be in A. If we now consider the two states, A and B, and allow a very large number of molecules to distribute themselves between these two states, the ratio of the numbers of molecules in A and B can be shown by statistics to be given by (1),

$$\frac{(A)}{(B)} = e^{-\Delta E/RT} \tag{1}$$

where e is the base of natural logarithms, T is the absolute temperature, and R is a proportionality constant (the gas law constant). Such a dis-

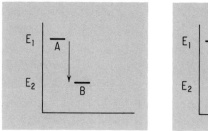

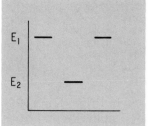

Fig. 8-1   Fig. 8-2

tribution of moleclues between states depends on the difference in energy between the states and on the absolute temperature. If ΔE is very large, the number of molecules in state A is very small, while as ΔE approaches zero the ratio (A)/(B) approaches 1. Notice that at very high temperatures the ratio also approaches 1, while at low temperatures it approaches zero. This equation gives the so-called Boltzmann distribution of molecules between states, and is one of the most useful of chemical equations.

If there are three states available to the molecules (A, B, C), then the Boltzmann distribution applies between each pair of states. Often one wishes to know the distribution of molecules between energies, and it sometimes happens that two or more states are degenerate, as in Fig. 8-2. The Boltzmann distribution applies between any two states as usual, but if the ratio of molecules with energy E_1 to those of energy E_2 is desired, the probability of having E_1 here will be twice as great as in the nondegenerate case depicted in Fig. 8-1. This probability factor must always be taken into account when considering the populations of degenerate systems, and this probability is measured by the entropy of the system.

We are usually not so much interested in the difference in energy between two molecular arrangements as we are in the total difference resulting from both energy and entropy. This total difference is called the *free energy* (G), and corresponds to the maximum available energy that can actually be obtained from a system. The free energy is related to the enthalpy (H),[†] the entropy (S), and the absolute temperature by the equation (2). The equilibrium constant (K) of a reaction is related to the

$$\Delta G = \Delta H - T \Delta S \qquad (2)$$

[†]The energy E is an appropriate quantity to describe one molecule when no degeneracy is possible. With an assemblage of molecules, E would still be an appropriate quantity if the system were maintained at a constant volume. Chemistry is ordinarily carried out on the surface of the earth, and at a constant (atmospheric) pressure rather than at constant volume. Some work is done against the atmosphere during most chemical reactions by expansion (or contraction) of the reaction system, and the enthalpy (H) is the energy (E) corrected for this work, and at constant pressure, $\Delta H = \Delta E + P \Delta V$.

standard free energy of the reaction (the free energy change for one mole reacting under standard conditions) by equation (3). For most chemical

$$-\Delta G^\circ = RT \ln K \qquad (3)$$

equilibria it is possible to calculate or to estimate ΔS from considerations of symmetry. Usually it is small enough that the ΔE for the reaction is not only a good approximation for ΔH, but it is a fairly good approximation for ΔG as well. A fair estimate of the equilibrium point for most reactions can therefore be made from the approximate relationship (4),

$$-\Delta E^\circ \approx RT \ln K \qquad (4)$$

and the ΔE° for the reaction is an approximately additive quantity obtained from bond energy tables such as Table 8-1. The use of these quan-

Table 8-1
SOME REPRESENTATIVE BOND STRENGTHS (kcal/mole)

H—H	104	F—F	37	C—H	99	C=O (ald.)	176
H—F	135	Cl—Cl	58	C—F	105	C=O (ket.)	179
H—Cl	103	Br—Br	46	C—Cl	79	C=C	146
H—Br	87	I—I	36	C—Br	66	C=C	200
H—I	71			C—I	57	C≡C	
H—N	93			C—O	84		
H—O	111			C—C	83		
				C—N	70		

tities can be illustrated as follows (from Table 8-1), taking as an example the reaction of hydrogen and fluorine to give hydrogen fluoride.

$$\begin{array}{ccccc} H-H & + & F-F & \longrightarrow & 2H-F \\ 104 & & 37 & & 2 \times 135 \end{array}$$

The amount of energy required to break the H—H and F—F bonds is 141 kcal/mole. When the atoms recombine to form H—F, 270 kcal/mole are liberated. The reaction is therefore exothermic by $(270 - 141) = 129$ kcal/mole; thus ΔE for the reaction is about -129 kcal/mole, and the approximate equilibrium constant for the reaction at $0°C$ is found from (4):

$$-129 \text{ kcal/mole} = (.002 \text{ kcal/mole}°C)(273°) \ln K$$

so $\ln K = 236$ and $K = 10^{103}$. The reaction therefore goes essentially 100% to completion.

The reaction

$$\begin{array}{ccccc} H-I & + & CH_3-I & \longrightarrow & I_2 & + & CH_4 \\ 71 & & 57 & & 36 & & 99 \end{array}$$

is exothermic by 7 kcal/mole, which again is enough to make the reaction proceed to well over 99% completion. By these methods the equilibrium constant K can be calculated approximately for almost any reaction.

The thermodynamics of chemical reactions is thus a relatively simple matter in principle, although in practice it can get rather involved with details. Unfortunately, the thermodynamics of a chemical reaction only tells us what kinds of molecules we will have at equilibrium; it doesn't tell us how to go about establishing equilibrium. If thermodynamics tells us a certain reaction will fail, there is no use trying it.[†] If, on the other hand, thermodynamics indicates that a reaction is favorable, then one has the practical chemical problem of making it actually occur.

8.2 KINETICS

If we are interested in the reaction $A \longrightarrow B$, and the thermodynamics of the reaction is favorable, the reaction may fail for either of two kinetic reasons. In a chemical reaction an existing bond is usually broken and a new one is formed, either in that order or simultaneously. To break a bond costs energy, although it may be recovered with interest later on. Consequently, almost all chemical reactions, as they proceed along the reaction coordinate from the starting state A to the product B, go through a geometric arrangement corresponding to an energy maximum ($A^{\ddagger}$), which is called the transition state (Fig. 8-3).

The equilibrium between A and B shown in Fig. 8-3 is determined by $\Delta G°$ as discussed previously, and since the quantity is negative, the reaction tends to proceed. How fast the reaction proceeds depends, however, on the *free energy of activation*, $\Delta G^{\ddagger}$. If $\Delta G^{\ddagger}$ is zero, the reaction will proceed as fast as the molecules can collide, which is almost instantaneously. If $\Delta G^{\ddagger}$ is extremely large, the reaction may proceed at a rate which is negligibly slow, and hence it may fail for practical purposes. Sometimes such a reaction can be accelerated with the aid of a catalyst. An example is the hydrogenation of ethylene: $CH_2{=}CH_2 + H_2 \longrightarrow CH_3{-}CH_3$. The reaction proceeds at an infinitesimal rate in the absence of a catalyst, but in the presence of platinum the reaction proceeds rapidly. The catalyst lowers $\Delta G^{\ddagger}$ by allowing us in effect to have a path around the mountain instead of having to go over the top. It does not affect the equilibrium point, however.

The other common cause of failure in attempting to carry out an organic reaction is due to the occurrence of side reactions. Suppose one is trying to convert A to B, and $\Delta G°$ is favorable, and $\Delta G^{\ddagger}$ is not so high as to prevent the reaction. It may be that A can also react to form another compound, C. If the reaction coordinate diagram for these reac-

[†] "No use trying it" under the conditions where it is predicted to fail. Often an unfavorable reaction can be tricked into working by shifting the equilibrium by precipitation of an insoluble material, evolution of a gas, etc.

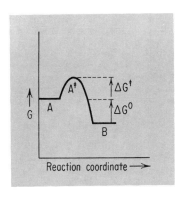

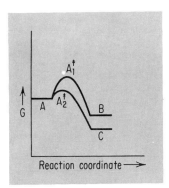

Fig. 8-3   Fig. 8-4

tions of A is as shown in Fig. 8-4, it will be difficult to form B, because C is formed more rapidly and is more stable. Typical organic compounds may react in many ways to give many different products. Thus the adjusting of the reaction variables (concentration, solvent, temperature, etc.) to obtain preferentially the desired reaction is as much an art as it is a science.

The reaction type we have discussed so far has been A $\longrightarrow$ B. Often we are interested in multi-step reactions: A $\longrightarrow$ B $\longrightarrow$ C $\longrightarrow$ D, etc. A reaction coordinate diagram can be constructed for the steps one by one, as in the particular example shown in Fig. 8-5. While the first step is unfavorable, if we can get to equilibrium, the starting material will be largely converted to the final product.

Suppose the reaction is of the type:

$$A + B \longrightarrow C$$

The rate at which the reaction will proceed can under no circumstances be faster than the rate at which molecules of A and B are able to collide.

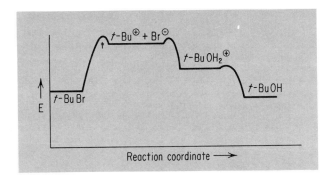

Fig. 8-5

For simple reactions in the gas phase, the rate of collision of molecules of A and B will have a certain value for specific concentrations of A and B. If we double the concentration of A, the collisions will take place twice as often. If we double the concentration of B, but keep the original concentration of A, the collisions will again take place twice as often. If we double both the concentrations of A and B, the collisions will take place four times as often. The rate of the reaction will therefore be proportional to the product of the concentrations of A and B. If we return to the original concentrations of A and B, but increase the temperature, the molecules will move faster and collide more often. If every collision between molecules A and B results in a reaction, then the rate of the reaction (or the rate of formation of C) will be the derivative of (C) with respect to time, and the *rate equation* is therefore

$$\frac{d(C)}{dt} = k(A)(B) \tag{5}$$

where k is a temperature dependent number called the specific rate constant for the reaction, a number which in principle can be calculated knowing the sizes of the molecules and their masses and velocities.

For reactions which have activation energies, the reaction will be found to proceed at a rate which is slower than expected from the value of k calculated. The free energy of activation is the minimum amount of free energy that the colliding molecules must have available for the reaction to be successful. In any assemblage of molecules there is a distribution of their energies about the most probable value. Thus some of the molecules will have very small energies, and when these molecules collide they will have insufficient energy to react and will simply undergo an elastic collision. The fraction of molecules which will have sufficient energy to react is given by (6):

$$\frac{(A')}{(A)} = e^{-\Delta G^{\ddagger}/RT} \tag{6}$$

In Fig. 8-6 is shown a plot of the population of molecules having a specific energy against the various possible energies for a given temperature (T_1). At a higher temperature (T_2) the most probable energy per molecule is higher, and the number of molecules having still higher energies is also greater. As can be seen from Fig. 8-6, at the lower temperature (T_1) only a small percentage of the molecules have sufficient energy to react upon collision (an energy greater than E') while at the higher temperature (T_2) the fraction with sufficient energy for reaction is much larger. It is thus found to be generally true that reactions proceed more rapidly at higher temperatures.

There is still one last requirement that must be fulfilled before two molecules will react. Even if they do collide, and even if they have sufficient

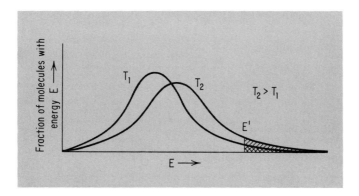

Fig. 8-6

energy for reaction, they can only react if their orientation in the collision is proper to lead to the reaction product. Some reactions have very little orientational requirement (atoms reacting with one another in the gas phase for example), while some reactions have such highly specific orientational requirements that even though the molecules collide with sufficient energy, millions of collisions may be necessary before a reaction occurs.

To more fully appreciate the principles developed so far in this chapter, it will be advantageous to examine some specific cases. As a simple, typical example, consider the reaction of methyl bromide with hydroxide ion in an aqueous solvent:

$$CH_3Br + OH^{\ominus} \longrightarrow CH_3OH + Br^{\ominus}$$

This reaction bears some obvious resemblance to the neutralization of an acid by a base to form a salt; here hydroxide ion (a base) is reacting to yield bromide ion (a salt). One might guess that the reaction would proceed essentially irreversibly in the direction indicated, and this is what actually happens. The reaction proceeds slowly at room temperature, but more rapidly if the temperature is increased. The reaction coordinate diagram is experimentally found to be as shown in Fig. 8-3, where state A in the figure corresponds to methyl bromide and hydroxide ion, and state B corresponds to methyl alcohol and bromide ion. The rate of the reaction is given by:

$$\frac{d(Br^{\ominus})}{dt} = k(CH_3Br)(OH^{\ominus})$$

A mechanism consistent with this reaction is a *displacement* process in which the hydroxide ion comes in from the side of the tetrahedron opposite that of the bromine, and pushes out the bromide ion with simultaneous inversion of the carbon atom (like an umbrella turning inside out).

This stereochemical change is referred to as a Walden inversion; studies

$$HO^{\ominus} + H\!-\!\!\overset{\displaystyle H}{\underset{\displaystyle H}{\diagdown}}\!\!C\!-\!Br \longrightarrow HO\text{-}\!\!\overset{\displaystyle H}{\underset{\displaystyle H}{\overset{\displaystyle H^{\ominus}}{\diagup}}}\!\!C\text{-}\!\!Br \longrightarrow HO\!-\!\!\overset{\displaystyle H}{\underset{\displaystyle H}{\diagup}}\!\!C\!\!-\!\!H + Br^{\ominus}$$

on optically active secondary bromides (and on optically active primary bromides of the type RCDH—X) have shown that these compounds react exclusively by Walden inversion. A reaction of this type is sometimes designated by the shorthand symbol S_N2 (substitution, nucleophilic, second order). Thus, the reaction involved a substitution (of bromine by hydroxyl) at carbon; the attacking agent is a nucleophile (nucleus seeker); and the rate law is second order (the product of two concentrations). Note that the product of the substances appearing in the rate expression $(CH_3BrOH^{\ominus})$ gives the formula of the transition state. The solvent plays some role in this reaction, since there is a redistribution of charge as the reaction proceeds, and the energy of electronic charge is affected by solvation. The effects are not very large, however, and the reaction will proceed at about the same rate in any solvent in which the reagents are soluble. The reaction is accelerated by about a factor of 3 for each 15° rise in temperature, which is more or less typical of chemical reactions in general.

A reaction which appears from the stoichiometry to be similar to the S_N2 reaction but which in fact is quite different is:

$$t\text{-BuBr} + OH^{\ominus} \longrightarrow t\text{-BuOH} + Br^{\ominus}$$

That the mechanism of this reaction is fundamentally different from the reaction of methyl bromide with base is indicated by the rate equation, which is found experimentally to be:

$$\frac{d(Br^{\ominus})}{dt} = k(t\text{-BuBr})$$

This reaction is seen to be first order. Hydroxide ion, although it appears in the net reaction, does not appear in the rate equation, which means that increasing the concentration of hydroxide ion does not increase the rate of reaction. Furthermore, the rate expression shows that hydroxide ion does not appear in the transition state. As was mentioned in Chapter 7, $CH_3^{\oplus}$ is an exceedingly unstable ion, while $t\text{-Bu}^{\oplus}$ is much more stable because of inductive and resonance effects. The mechanism for the reaction of t-butyl bromide with hydroxide ion is in fact as follows:

$$t\text{-Bu}\!-\!Br \xrightarrow{H_2O} Br^{\ominus} + t\text{-Bu}^{\oplus} \xrightarrow{:OH_2} t\text{-Bu}\!-\!\!\overset{\displaystyle \oplus}{\underset{\displaystyle H}{O}}\!\!-\!H \xrightarrow{OH^{\ominus}} t\text{-Bu}\!-\!OH + H_2O$$

The rate of this reaction is determined by what happens in the first step, and the transition state has a geometry similar to that of t-butyl bromide, except the C—Br bond is stretched. Hydroxide ion becomes involved only in a later stage, and thus it comes into the net reaction but not into the rate expression. The reaction coordinate diagram for this reaction is as shown in Fig. 8-5. The shorthand notation for a first order reaction of this kind is $S_N 1$. Since this reaction involves, in the transition state, the creation of ions from a neutral particle, its rate is very sensitive to solvent. A solvent of high dielectric constant which will stabilize the ionic charge being generated in the transition state will make the reaction go very much faster than will a non-polar solvent. In the gas phase (very low dielectric constant) the reaction is so slow that for practical purposes it does not proceed. The effect of solvent on a reaction can be exceedingly important but is often difficult to understand quantitatively.

We have now discussed in some detail all of the features which are at the present time thought to be important for the understanding of the structures of organic moleclues, and we have briefly outlined a few of the relationships between structure and reactivity. Succeeding volumes in this series will discuss the chemical properties of these compounds which result from their structures and will present in more detail the physical methods used for the determination of organic structures.

8.3 PROBLEMS

1. Draw reaction coordinate diagrams for the reaction of (a) n-butyl chloride with hydroxide ion; (b) t-butyl bromide with hydroxide ion; (c) acetylene with hydrogen both with and without a catalyst.

2. Write the mechanism for the reaction of hydroxide ion with (a) n-butyl chloride; (b) t-butyl bromide. Show how these mechanisms are consistent with the kinetics of the reactions.

3. From the data in Table 8-1, calculate the energy changes for the following reactions:

(a) $CH_3CH_2CH_2CH_2OH + HBr \longrightarrow CH_3CH_2CH_2CH_2Br + H_2O$

(b) $(CH_3)_2C{=}O + H_2O \longrightarrow (CH_3)_2C\overset{\displaystyle OH}{\underset{\displaystyle OH}{\big\langle}}$

(c) $CH_3CH_2CH_2Br + HI \longrightarrow CH_3CH_2CH_2{-}I + HBr$

(d) $CH_2{=}CH_2 + H_2 \longrightarrow CH_3{-}CH_3$

4. (a) Calculate which tautomer will be stable:

$$CH_3{-}C\overset{\displaystyle O}{\underset{\displaystyle H}{\big\langle}} \quad \text{or} \quad CH_2{=}CHOH$$

(b) Do you expect the same situation with the compounds

Why?

SUGGESTED READINGS

Elementary Chemical Thermodynamics, by B. H. Mahan, New York, W. A. Benjamin, Inc., 1963, and *How Chemical Reactions Occur*, by E. L. King, New York, W. A. Benjamin, Inc., 1963, are good introductions to thermodynamics and kinetics respectively. *The Influence of Functional Groups on the Properties of Organic Compounds*, by O. L. Chapman, Englewood Cliffs, N. J., Prentice-Hall, Inc., 1964 continues the development of the subject of organic chemistry begun in this volume, and *Investigation of Organic Reactions*, by R. Stewart, Englewood Cliffs, N. J., Prentice-Hall, Inc., (1966) discusses the details of such investigations.

Index